EMPATH & NARCISSIST ABUSE

HOW TO UNDERSTAND AND OVERCOME FEELINGS OF ABUSE

MYSTIC MAE

ABOUT THE AUTHOR

Mystic Mae is a senior coach at Mindset Mastership, a life coaching business based in London, England.

Mindset Mastership teaches clients how human behavior really works. Through our teaching, we have helped clients worldwide gain a better advantage, to develop themselves, and achieve more from life.

We're in the changing lives business.

YOU DESERVE TO BE SPIRITUALLY FULFILLED

Introducing *Basics of Spiritual Living - Baby Steps to Living a Spiritually Fulfilled Life.*

With this short eBook, readers will gain the foundations of spiritual living and be able to take small steps towards achieving a spiritually fulfilled life.

To get this FREE short eBook, email me at:

mysticmaeauthor@gmail.com

WANT A COPY OF MY NEW EBOOK?

Email me:
mysticmaeauthor@gmail.com

FOLLOW US ON INSTAGRAM

https://www.instagram.com/mindsetmastership/

© Copyright 2022 by (United Arts Publishing, England.) - All rights reserved.

This document is geared towards providing exact and reliable information in regard to the topic and issue covered. The publication is sold with the idea that the publisher is not required to render accounting, officially permitted, or otherwise, qualified services. If advice is necessary, legal or professional, a practised individual in the profession should be ordered.

- From a Declaration of Principles which was accepted and approved equally by a Committee of the American Bar Association and a Committee of Publishers and Associations.

In no way is it legal to reproduce, duplicate, or transmit any part of this document in either electronic means or in printed format. Recording of this publication is strictly prohibited and any storage of this document is not allowed unless with written permission from the publisher. All rights reserved.

The information provided herein is stated to be truthful and consistent, in that any liability, in terms of inattention or otherwise, by any usage or abuse of any policies, processes, or directions contained within is the solitary and utter responsibility of the recipient reader. Under no circumstances will any legal responsibility or blame be held against the publisher for any reparation, damages, or monetary loss due to the information herein, either directly or indirectly.

Respective authors own all copyrights not held by the publisher.

The information herein is offered for informational purposes solely, and is universal as so. The presentation of the information is without contract or any type of guarantee assurance.

The trademarks that are used are without any consent, and the publication of the trademark is without permission or backing by the trademark owner. All trademarks and brands within this book are for clarifying purposes only and are the owned by the owners themselves, not affiliated with this document.

PERSONAL SELF-GROWTH POWER GROUP

To help reinforce the learning's from our books, I strongly suggest you join our well-informed powerhouse community on Facebook. Here, you will connect and share with other like-minded people to support your journey and help you grow.

CLICK THE LINK BELOW:

https://www.facebook.com/wellnessmastership/

**DISCOVER A
NEW & BETTER YOU**

DO YOU NEED HELP IMPROVING YOUR SPIRITUAL CONNECTION?

Mystic Mae's books offer comprehensive guidance and tools to help you connect with your spirit guides and gain a greater understanding of life's mysteries and yourself.

Discover the possibilities waiting for you through her other books. Get started on your spiritual journey today!

The Author's Other Books:

Animal Spirit Guides; The Shaman's Ultimate Spirit Animal Guidebook, Meanings & Attributes, Connect and Channel Your Power Animal, A Guidebook to Shamanism, Shamanic Animal Magic and Medicine

Akashic Records for Beginners, Spiritual Guidance & Higher Consciousness, Find Purpose to Your Souls Journey: Unlock The Secret Key to Manifesting The Law of Attraction

Ancestral Veneration: Connecting with your Ancestors, Honoring the Heart of your Spirit Guides, Spiritual Families & Guardian Angels: Connect with Angels, Healing Trauma & Find Your Souls Journey

Vibrate Higher, Daily Reading | Raising Consciousness & Spiritual Awareness: The Complete Vibrational Guide, The Secret Key to Manifesting The Law of Attraction

Kabbalah Beginners Guide the Secret Knowledge, Tree of Life, Jewish Mysticism, Qabalah Magick and the Spiritual Life

*"Wherever you go, go
with all your heart."*
— **Confucius**

MASTERSHIP BOOKS

UK | USA | Canada | Ireland | Australia
India | New Zealand | South Africa | China

Mastership Books is part of the United Arts Publishing House group of companies based in London, England, UK.

First published by Mastership Books (London, UK), 2022

Text Copyright © United Arts Publishing

All rights reserved. Without limiting the rights under copyright reserved above, no part of this publication may be reproduced, stored in or introduced into a retrieval system, or transmitted, in any form or by any means (electronic, mechanical, photocopying, recording or otherwise), without the prior written permission of both the copyright owner and the above publisher of this book.

Cover design by Rich © United Arts Publishing (UK)
Text and internal design by Rich © United Arts Publishing (UK)

Image credits reserved.
Colour separation by Spitting Image Design Studio

Printed and bound in Great Britain
National Publications Association of Britain
London, England, United Kingdom.

Paper design UAP
A723.5

Title: Empath & Narcissist Abuse

Design, Bound & Printed:
London, England,
Great Britain.

Mindfulness, Meditation, Spirituality Books

GET A FREE AUDIOBOOK

EMAIL SUBJECT LINE:

"EMPATH NARCISSIST"

TO

mysticmaesauthor@gmail.com

CONTENTS

Introduction   xxiii

1. WHAT IS AN EMPATH? AM I ONE?   1
    How to Tell if You're an Empath   1
    Empath Tests   2
    How to Tell if You're Empathetic   3
    Having Empathy Has Many Advantages   3
    The Difficulties of Being an Empath   4
    Being Protective of Yourself as an Empath   5
    Find Some Personal Time   5
    Choose Wisely Whom You Spend Time With   5
    How to Increase Empathy   6
    Key Findings   6

2. 13 SIGNS THAT YOU'RE EMPATHETIC   8
    13 Signs of Empathy   9
    You Are a Narcissist if You Display 8 Terrifying Symptoms   13
    Am I a narcissist?   13
    8 Terrifying Symptoms of a Narcissist   14
    Key Findings   17

3. DISTINCTIVE EMPATH TRAITS   18
    Let's look at it, so you will know what to expect the next time you run into this type of individual.   18
    Two fast indicators of a very intuitive empath are listed below: 24
    Prioritizing oneself   27
    13 Empath Indicators   27
    13 Indicators that You're Empathetic   28
    Key Findings   31

4. SEVEN EMPATH TYPES YOU SHOULD KNOW   32
    Emotional Empath   32
    Physical Empath   33
    Intuitive Empath   33
    Plant Empath   33

Animal Empath	33
Empath Earth	34
Heyoka Empath	34
Key Findings	34

5. SIX EMPATHS: GIFTS AND DIFFICULTIES — 36

Let's look at each sort of empath in more depth, including their special gifts, and their difficulties. — 37

1. The Empath with Emotions — 37
What Talents Do Emotional Empaths Possess? — 37
The Difficulties of Being an Emotional Empath — 37
How to Manage Being an Emotional Empathetic Person — 38
2. The Physical Empath — 38
What Talents do Physical Empaths Possess? — 38
The Obstacles Facing a Physical Empath — 39
How to Manage Your Physical Empathy — 39
3. Geomantic Empaths — 39
What Talents do Geomantic Empaths Possess? — 40
The Obstacles Facing a Geomantic Empath — 40
How to Manage Your Geomantic Empathy — 40
4. Earth Empaths — 41
What Talents do Earth Empaths Possess? — 41
Problems With Being an Earth Empath — 41
How Should I Manage my Earth Empathy? — 42
5. Intuitive Empaths — 42
What Talents Does an Empath Intuitive Possess? — 42
Difficulties of Being an Empathic Intuitive — 42
How Should I Manage My Intuitive Empath Status? — 43
6. Animal Empaths — 43
What Qualities do Animal Empaths Possess? — 43
Problems With Being an Animal Empath — 44
How Should I Manage my Empathy for Animals? — 44
Can you have many empathic types? — 44
Which Type Are You? — 44
Key Findings — 45

6. THE SYMPTOMS OF AN ABUSIVE RELATIONSHIP — 46

Signs of an Abusive Relationship — 47
Communication Monitoring — 47
Isolation — 47

Financial management	48
Coercion	48
Emotional manipulation	48
Physical violence	49
How to Handle an Abusive Relationship	49
Abusive Behaviors	49
Understanding the Symptoms of Emotional Abuse	53
Emotional abuse: what is it?	53
Embarrassment, dismissal, and criticism	54
Control and shame	55
They try to get you to do what they want by:	55
Denial, blaming, and accusations	57
Isolation and neglect of emotions	58
They could employ the following strategies:	59
How to handle emotional assault	60
Key Findings	61

7. TIPS FOR GETTING OVER NARCISSISTIC ABUSE — 64

Recognize the abuse and accept it	65
Establish clear boundaries for yourself.	65
Get your identity back.	67
What it might resemble:	67
Practice self-compassion	68
Be aware that your feelings might linger.	68
Take care of yourself.	69
Chat with others.	69
Obtain expert assistance	70
Key Findings	71

8. HOW TO DEAL WITH ABUSE: A GUIDE (PHYSICAL, EMOTIONAL, OR VERBAL) — 72

The Best Ways to Handle Physical Abuse	72
The Best Ways to Handle Emotional Abuse	75
How to Respond to Verbal Harassment	77
How Do I Establish Boundaries?	80
Safety is a Right for All Women	80
Boundaries Safeguard emotional abuse victims.	80
How do Boundaries Appear?	81
Boundaries Protect Victims and Make Sure That Abusers Don't Change.	81

Set boundaries to protect your safety rather than to influence your partner.	82
BTR Aids Victims in Setting and Upholding Boundaries	82
What is The Purpose of a Boundary?	82
Boundaries That Prevent Damage	83
The BTR Boundaries Model	83
Definition of a Boundary	83
Statements are merely statements and cannot protect you.	84
Make a list of your safety concerns.	84
Setting boundaries is different from identifying safety issues.	85
Choose appropriate actions based on your safety concerns.	85
Physical and mental actions: Limits are Actions.	85
Consider The Property Line as an Example.	85
Establish Boundaries That Meet Your Needs for Safety	86
What is a Good Boundary for YOU?	86
Benchmark – What is it?	87
Boundaries Done Backwards	88
Limits Have Two Components	89
Pay Attention to Manipulation	89
Limits are Godly and Healthy	89
Protecting Yourself From Danger	90
Setting Boundaries vs. Identifying Safety Issues	90
A Boundary is a Wall That Reduces the Effects of the Damage	91
Boundaries are not Requests	91
There are two steps to using the BTR model for boundaries:	92
Is a Boundary a Protective Barrier?	92
You are powerless over what the abuser does.	92
Boundaries Reduce His Negative Behavior's Impact	93
Why do Boundaries Exist and How Can I Protect Myself?"	93
The actual harm is significantly diminished.	93
Key Findings	94

9. WHAT IS CODEPENDENCY? 96
    Codependency: the APA Definition 96
    Causes of Codependency 97
    Signs of Codependency 98
    Reasons Codependency is Dangerous 99
    Getting Rid of Codependency 99
    When you start that adventure, do your best to follow these guidelines: 100
    Key Findings 101

10. IMPROVING EMOTIONAL INTELLIGENCE (EQ) 102
    What exactly is EQ or emotional intelligence? 102
    Four characteristics frequently used to characterize emotional intelligence: 103
    What makes emotional IQ so crucial? 103
    What EQ entails: 104
    Four essential abilities to develop emotional intelligence (EQ) 104
    Emotional and social intelligence are allies of mindfulness. 107
    Key Findings 108

11. SIX SELF-CARE STRATEGIES FOR DEALING WITH TRAUMA 110
    Key Findings 113

12. A MANUAL FOR MINDFUL SELF-CARE PRACTICE 115
    Self-Care: What Is It? 115
    The Development of Self-Care 116
    How to Create a Movement for Self-Care 116
    Why is Self-Care Important? 118
    You Need a Self-Care Plan for 3 Reasons 118
    Making a Self-Care Plan: a Guide 119
    Using Self-Care Techniques 120
    Several Techniques for Self-Care Today 120
    Learning to Say, "I Need Help," is the Most Courageous Self-Care Act. 121
    Three Self-Care Techniques to Take Back Your Healing Time 122
    Name-it-to-Tame-It: The Confession Statement 122
    The Pre-Ask: requesting assistance or room before you require it 122

The Kindness Factor: Remember that people enjoy lending a hand.	123
How to Take Care of Your Emotions in Tough Times	123
How to Take Care of Your Emotions	123
How to Control Tough Feelings Without Suppressing Them	124
The Shameful Truth About Self-Care	125
Self-Care Techniques to Apply Daily	126
Reevaluating Self-Care in the Face of the Pandemic	126
Four Self-Care Practices for the Workplace	128
Key Findings	129
13. KEEPING A JOURNAL	**131**
Security first	131
What topic should I choose?	131
How can journaling benefit me?	132
The emotional advantages of journaling	132
THE IMPACTS OF KEEPING A JOURNAL	132
Key Findings	133
14. 8 KEY WAYS TO LIVE AS AN EMPOWERED EMPATH	**134**
Key Findings	137
CONCLUSION	140

INTRODUCTION

Mental health has the potential to become an even more severe problem than the dreaded disease diabetes. People are feeling the pain of being alone, their health is getting worse, and they suffer from breakdowns. They want to hide away in their little caves where no one can hurt them, and it's a big deal for society at large.

Some people are stuck inside their minds and constantly feed their souls with hate and misery. This makes it easy for people to hurt each other, which is why they must be reminded that their actions are wrong and not the norm. Abuse in the modern world is real and hurts. We are just now realizing that we have the right to protect ourselves from people who want to hurt us. Here are some ways to stop the damage and misfortunes that result. This book examines what you can do to prevent abuse from draining your energy.

Abuse is an invasion of privacy because the person hurting you is in your life and doesn't like you the way you are for some reasons. It may just be their nature. They are telling you that you have to change. They often pull at your heartstrings to hurt your feelings and get you to give in. They use your family and friends against you and say things to make you think that others are unhappy with you too.

They want you to believe that most people are against you and

Introduction

the problem is worse than you think. It would be an immense mistake to believe such nonsense and accept the abuse. Some things work, but keep in mind that abusive people are stewing in their juices about some hot issue they have entirely made up that keeps boiling.

Empaths are exceptionally empathic or more empathetic than average. When you have a high level of empathy, your anxiety can be exacerbated by the emotions of those around you. Experts have established a link between empathy and depression. Mindfully releasing emotions enables you to transition from the "feeling" stage to the "acting" stage of compassion. Only 2% of the population can be classified as empaths or "highly sensitive." They are the people who tend to garner abuse.

Being an empath does not mean that you need to bear the burden of the entire world on your shoulders. Empaths can benefit greatly from learning to be mindful through formal mindfulness meditation or developing a greater awareness of themselves. Empathy is the decision to express solidarity over a traumatic event, whether shared or not. According to reports, 2% of people in the U.K., for example, identify as empaths, yet they are more likely to blame their shortcomings on how they feel. A big step toward overcoming what they mistakenly believe to be generalized anxiety disorder is realizing that you can sense other people's emotions and take on their abuse.

Empathy stops being a burden and can be used as a talent. Understanding someone else's emotions allows you to know how they feel inside. Your empathic capacity develops into a talent you can employ to help those around you. Being an empath means you'll inevitably draw those who need your help the most. So there are two sides to the empath coin: your gift and the resulting abuse.

It can be tempting to try to downplay the severity of your experiences. Low self-esteem, anxiety, sadness, and a sense of helplessness are common problems among survivors. Some individuals who experience emotional abuse go on to experience a nervous collapse. When the effects of emotional abuse become intolerable, a loss of function occurs. Nervous breakdowns are characterized by a

Introduction

decreased capacity for self-care and a loss of the ability to engage in social and professional activities.

You may suffer sleep issues, paranoia, hallucinations, obsessive thoughts, and physical symptoms such as gastrointestinal discomfort, shaking, and muscle tightness. Comprehensive care in a residential facility is frequently the best choice to ensure quick healing in a secure setting. A nervous breakdown is not a mental health diagnosis, but it could be a clue that you have a mental illness. You might be hesitant to talk about the complicated emotions that survivors frequently experience. Nonverbal, somatic, and holistic therapies can create a space, where you can start the healing process without discussing your experiences in detail.

Read on to master, understand, and overcome abuse.

Dear Reader,

As independent authors, it's often difficult to gather reviews compared with much bigger publishers.

Therefore, please leave a review on the platform where you bought this book.

KINDLE:

[LEAVE A REVIEW HERE < click here >](#)

Many thanks,

Author Team

1

WHAT IS AN EMPATH? AM I ONE?

An empath takes in and deeply processes the moods and emotions of those around them. Empaths experience the feelings of another person at a profound emotional level. Beyond empathy, which is the capacity to comprehend the feelings of another, they can ascertain what others are feeling. Being an empath involves genuinely embracing those emotions. However, they may in the process experience abuse.

Even though many people claim to be true empaths—individuals who can access and absorb the emotions of those around them—science remains divided on the subject. We are aware of "mirror neurons" in the brain that may enable us to mimic the emotions of others we touch. It appears that some individuals have more mirror neurons than others, indicating the possibility of real empaths.

How to Tell if You're an Empath

What signs might indicate that you are an empath? Common characteristics include:

- **Empathy"** Undoubtedly, some people have a higher propensity for empathy than others. In addition to persons who appear to be utterly cut off from the feelings of those around them, we have all encountered individuals who are simply excellent at reading our emotions.

- **Intuition:** Additionally, empaths frequently have excellent intuition; they follow their gut feelings, and believe in their instincts when making decisions. Due to their keen awareness of other people's emotions, they may notice nuances or indications that could inform their choices.

- **Caring:** People who identify as empaths frequently have deep compassion for others. Because they understand the needs, wants, and concerns of others, empaths may dedicate themselves to making sure those around them are cared for and content. People might categorize them as compassionate or warm-hearted as a result. However, this propensity can occasionally make it difficult for empaths to establish boundaries with others.

- **Sensitivity:** Empaths are emotionally wise and have a propensity for picking up on environmental cues. This implies that individuals might be more sensitive to physical stimuli such as sights, sounds, and smells that others might miss. As a result, an empath could be more readily offended by particular smells or distracted by external noises. Their attraction to certain conditions may include abuse.

Empath Tests

How do you gauge your empathy, assuming it is a spectrum, with some people being highly empathic and others (psychopaths) completely devoid? At what moment did you first recognize that you were an empath?

How to Tell if You're Empathetic

Consider assessing your interpersonal skills and physical and emotional reactions to significant events in your presence. There's a strong possibility you're an empath if you find yourself answering "yes" to most or all of the following questions:
- Do you frequently take on the tension of others?
- Have you ever been criticized for having too many feelings?
- Do you experience anxiety in crowded places?
- Would you consider yourself to be sympathetic?

You can identify if you are an empath by taking one of the many tests designed by experts. How often do you feel like an outsider? Judith Orloff, Ph.D. asks some questions while self-proclaimed empath Tara Meyer-Robson inquires whether you have difficulty processing news or find sad movies too much to bear. But there is no universally accepted test to determine whether a person is an empath, so the answer to that question is totally up to the individual.

Having Empathy Has Many Advantages

Is it advantageous to be an empath? Being acutely sensitive to other people's emotional experiences has clear advantages. You should be better equipped to support and take care of the people who are special to you if you can tap into the emotions of those around you.

Even if they don't express it, when you are aware of another person's feelings of sadness, loneliness, or fear, you are more equipped to support them and gain their trust so that they will come to trust you in the future. This can improve your relationships and make you a better friend and spouse.

This sensitivity also enables you to recognize a liar from a mile away. Empaths are hard to trick or influence, so they don't have to worry about being taken advantage of. And when they are, it's not because they completely missed the signs but because they disregarded their first impressions of someone.

The Difficulties of Being an Empath

Being overly sensitive to other people's feelings undoubtedly has drawbacks. We have already hinted at abuse. Most of the research on empaths argues that because they are like emotional sponges, they are quickly overwhelmed in crowded places or emotionally charged occasions (like weddings and funerals). It's easy to envision how quickly that could get wearying.

Empaths may find it challenging to relax if they continuously drag around other people's feelings. If they can't find a means to balance the outside inputs they are constantly receiving, empaths may have trouble sleeping or keeping up their mental health.

Finally, some people find it unsettling that you seem to be able to skim them. Your good intentions may make you feel that everyone wants to have their lives laid bare for you, but this is not the case. Some people may find your intrusion into their sentiments and emotions undesired and intrusive.

Pros

- You can support someone emotionally.
- You are aware of it when someone requires assistance.
- A good match will be obvious.

Cons

- You frequently feel emotionally spent.
- It could be challenging to find time for yourself.
- Some people feel that reading their minds is intrusive.

Being Protective of Yourself as an Empath

It's critical to understand how to safeguard your psyche and isolate yourself from the outside world if you identify as an empath and frequently take on the emotions of others, not to mention their abuse. This will allow you to breathe, heal, and experience your own emotions.

Find Some Personal Time

Protection can entail time to be alone in a natural setting, away from people and their stressors. Another option is finding music or a meditation regimen to help you refocus and find your center.

Empaths also need to practice learning when and how to erect personal walls to prevent themselves from continually and quickly absorbing the emotions of those around them. It will be complex because empaths are motivated to help and probably need to learn how to set boundaries. However, setting sound boundaries is essential for everyone's mental health and well-being—possibly even more so for empaths. When the emotional input from others becomes overwhelming, you can improve your capacity to do the same by learning to concentrate and ignore distractions.

Choose Wisely Whom You Spend Time With

You'll probably discover that some people are better off keeping a distance from. Being with toxic and abusive people for an extended period can feel like poisoning since empaths absorb others' emotions, positive and negative. There are certain people you can't assist and others you should avoid at all costs. Setting appropriate limits is a great strategy to protect your mental health.

Asking a professional for assistance is always a good idea. You may need to build techniques to help you deal with issues if you frequently feel exhausted or overwhelmed by the emotions you encounter beyond your front door. With the help of an experienced mental health professional, you may achieve your full potential as a happy, healthy person. You will learn how to avoid and counter abuse.

When you have the emotional capacity to assist and care for people who need it most, you can learn how to apply your empathic abilities.

How to Increase Empathy

In spite of the potential for abuse, empathy is a great quality. You can take action to become more empathic in your daily life if you want to develop your empathic abilities.

- Show concern for others. Start observing how other people act, including their words and facial expressions. Talk to them and give them your full attention when they speak.
- Try putting yourself in another person's shoes. Understanding a problem from someone else's perspective is the essence of empathy. It enables you to experience their feelings genuinely, given their circumstances. Naturally, empaths can accomplish this, but you may also improve your own capacity for empathy by deliberately imagining yourself in another person's shoes.
- Be approachable. Making yourself open to others' sentiments is crucial if you want others to open up to you. Talk about your sentiments and allow others the freedom to do the same.

Key Findings

- An empath takes in and processes the moods and emotions of those around them. Common characteristics of empaths include empathy, compassion, and intuition.

Empaths are emotionally wise and have a propensity for picking up on environmental cues, such as sights, sounds, and smells missed by others. Being acutely sensitive to other people's emotional experiences has clear advantages. Empaths are hard to trick or influence, so they don't have to worry about being taken advantage of.

- Having empathy can improve your relationships and make you a better friend and spouse. Some people may find your intrusion into their sentiments and emotions undesired and intrusive. Empaths need to practice learning when and how to erect personal walls and avoid abuse. This can be complex because empaths are motivated to help and probably need to learn how to set boundaries. Some people are better off keeping a distance because empaths can absorb other people's emotions.
- Understanding a problem from someone else's perspective is the essence of empathy. You can take action to become more empathic in your daily life if you want to develop empathic abilities.

2

13 SIGNS THAT YOU'RE EMPATHETIC

How does one find out whether they are an empath? You already know that an empath is a person who is extraordinarily sensitive to the emotions of those around them—to the point that they experience these feelings themselves. Empaths have a unique perspective on the world because they have a deep awareness of others, their emotional needs, and their pain points.

But it goes beyond feelings. Empaths are capable of experiencing physical discomfort and abuse in addition to sensing another person's goals or source of motivation. In other words, empaths appear to pick up on what people around them are going through.

Although many HSPs are also empaths, there may be a distinction. One of the four characteristics that define an HSP is a high level of empathy, and HSPs are also highly sensitive to a wide range of stimuli and emotions. Although most empaths are probably also susceptible, not all people with high sensitivity levels are empaths.

How do you recognize one of them? Here are 13 indicators.

13 Signs of Empathy

1. You adopt the feelings of other individuals as your own. This is the most fundamental quality of an empath. No matter how close to you someone is, even if they believe they are not showing it, you are sure to notice it right away. Furthermore, you can genuinely experience the emotion as your own, basically "absorbing" or "sponging up" the feeling.

There is some disagreement regarding how this operates. The area of the brain that interprets emotional cues from others determines what they may think or feel is extremely active in high levels of empathy. In other words, if you're an empath, you can pick up on subtle shifts in expression, body language, or voice tone that others overlook and know exactly how someone is feeling.

But because the same mirror neurons are firing, you will experience the emotion as if it were your own. That can be a wonderful gift, but it can also be draining and overpowering.

2. When in public, you occasionally feel abrupt, intense emotions. You can detect other people's emotions in group settings and one-on-one conversations. When there are other people around, it can occur at any time without prior notice.

Going into public places might be difficult if you're an empath since you might find yourself suddenly overcome with a feeling that seems to come from "nowhere" or, more precisely, from someone else there.

3. You care a lot about a room's "vibe." Empaths are susceptible to the "feel" or environment of their surroundings, which should come as no surprise. They thrive in environments of tranquility and peace because they internalize those attributes. Likewise while they draw abuse, they detest it. For the same reason, peaceful settings like gardens, beautiful bedrooms, and museum halls can transform empaths. This is similar to how hectic or unpleasant circumstances quickly drain an empath's energy.

4. You are aware of people's perspectives. Absorbing other people's emotions, according to expert Dr. Judith Orloff, is the fundamental characteristic of an empath. After all, empaths can learn to "absorb" emotions less frequently, but some empaths hardly ever do. However, empaths can all detect it intuitively, even when people have difficulty expressing themselves. After all, at its core, empathy is about connecting with and comprehending other people. This is what it means to have the ability to tell where someone is coming from.

5. Individuals look to you for guidance. Empaths are regularly sought out by their friends for guidance, support, and encouragement because of their keen perception. But bad people know who they can abuse. The fact that empaths also have a propensity for attentive listening and will frequently wait patiently for someone to finish speaking before emotionally responding is helpful. If this describes you, you know that it can sometimes be challenging. Some people take it for granted and only sometimes appreciate the time and effort it takes to listen and offer advice.

6. Watching tragic or violent events on TV can render you helpless. Even if a terrible incident isn't happening to you, an empath nevertheless feels it deeply throughout their entire body. It is possible to "go through" the pain of losing someone or something even if you are thousands of miles away or if the event is fictitious - as on television. At times, this response might be utterly overwhelming. Empaths, like HSPs, could find it difficult to watch violent or tragic films, even if others find them riveting.

. . .

7. Your love for animals, children, and pets is intense. Everyone agrees that puppies and kittens are attractive and infants are adorable little miracles, but those feelings seem to be considerably stronger for an empath. You might be powerless to stop yourself from swooning over someone's cute youngster or squatting down to give a pet some love. Your response could be considered "over the top" by some; but how could anyone not feel this way? This is one of the numerous benefits of being an empath. Your emotions are all on high, even the good ones. You are vulnerable and susceptible to abuse.

8. You might sense people's emotions and their bodily ailments. When someone is ill or hurt, you could even experience the illness as though it were your own. This goes beyond having empathy or worry for someone and includes experiencing physical discomfort in the same bodily regions, such as pain, tightness, or soreness. Your empathic brain is transmitting the experience the other person must have into your own body and replicating it.

It can be painful, if not downright crippling. Most empaths undoubtedly do not enjoy having this "talent". However, it's also the reason empaths make such superb caring persons. Without this talent, they wouldn't be able to empathize with someone who is suffering or provide them with the comfort they require.

It makes sense that empaths are drawn to professions like nursing, medicine, caring for the elderly, or healing. It would be unexpected for you not to desire action if you could feel everyone else's suffering.

9. Being in close relationships can make you feel too much. Everyone experiences difficulties in their relationships. Imagine how difficult obstacles will be if you detect every little mood swing, annoyance, and, yes, even lie from your partner. Positive feelings can occasionally become debilitating, making you feel like the relationship would "engulf" you. Sounds recognizable?

But it goes beyond this. The shared atmosphere is another challenge once you start living together. For an empath, a cohabiting partner's "energy" is always present and can almost feel intrusive. A spouse alters how empaths regard their houses as a place of refuge, where they may escape the continual pressure on their emotional senses.

Although some empaths opt to remain single, others learn to adjust. They might do this by having a room designated as their own space or—and this is crucial—looking for a spouse who respects their limits. The bad news is that they often live with abuse for far too long.

10. You're a lying detector on foot. Sure, there have probably been moments when someone has tricked you. But even then, you were aware right away that you were acting against your better judgment. It's practically impossible for someone to conceal their genuine intentions because empaths can read even the most minor social clues. You can tell if someone isn't being entirely honest — or if they look shifty — even if you don't know what they want. Why then do empaths so often engender abuse?

11. You need to comprehend why leaders wouldn't prioritize their teams. Many managers and group leaders blatantly ignore the needs of their staff. If you're an empath, this is more than simply impolite or bothersome; it is a sign of leadership failure. This is partly because empaths make excellent leaders; and when they do, it's always through listening to the team and bringing people together around common objectives. Empaths are frequently considerate and sensitive, ensuring that every team member feels heard. Not only are people happier as a result, but they also make better decisions since they have all the facts.

. . .

12. **You can heal and have a calming impact on other individuals.** It is real. People seek out empaths for assistance and feel at ease in their company. In fact, during trying times, people frequently unintentionally seek out their most understanding companions. You may create and apply this to truly heal individuals by assisting them in overcoming heavy emotional burdens and destructive behaviors. But if you genuinely want to make a difference, you must accept your ability and not try to hide your sensitivity and empathy.

Above all avoid being someone's punching bag.

13. **When you witness someone in distress, you cannot help but want to assist them.** Can you pass someone in need without thinking about what you can do to help? Do you find it challenging to put aside your empathy for others when "you have a job to do?" If the answer is no, even at times of stress or when you're busy, there's a reasonable probability that you're an empath. And for this reason, empaths are such an essential component of the fascinating mosaic of the human race. An empath cannot help but notice and respond to the needs of others since people are the brightest things on their radar. That is where an empath's capacity for healing originates, and our world could use more of it.

You Are a Narcissist if You Display 8 Terrifying Symptoms

Although a licensed mental health professional can only diagnose narcissistic personality disorder (NPD), many people overcomplicate figuring out whether they know a narcissist. We focus on this type of personality as a clear contrast to an empath.

Am I a narcissist?

Although no precise scientific methods, blood tests, or X-rays can determine whether you or someone you know has NPD, it is feasible to assess narcissism in a person by searching for telltale behaviors, attitudes, and responses to others.

8 Terrifying Symptoms of a Narcissist

1. **Having a strong desire for control and perfection.** Narcissists have a severe need for perfection in everything. They expect you to be faultless and perfect and for everything to go as planned. The narcissist's constant complaining and dissatisfaction stem from their obsession with perfection. If they don't get it, they can become abusive.

2. **Feeling as though the laws don't apply to you.** The narcissist is superior to everyone else in their world because it is divided into good and bad, superior and inferior, and right and wrong. Narcissists must do everything their way, own everything, and control everyone. They need to be the top dogs in terms of quality, accuracy, and skill.

3. **Taking no accountability and instead blaming and diverting to others.** Despite their desire for control, narcissists never want to take responsibility for outcomes unless they get their way in every single instance. The narcissist assigns all blame to others when things don't go as planned; they feel criticized or less than ideal. They may hold a group (all law enforcement) or an individual (their parents) responsible when they feel they cannot act as they choose when they desire to and in the manner they choose. This is when their innate bent toward abuse appears.

4. **Lacking empathy.** Narcissists struggle to understand the nature of feelings and have little capacity for empathy. They typically lack empathy for others and tend to be selfish and self-absorbed. Narcissists rarely consider other people's feelings and assume that everyone

thinks and feels the same way they do. Additionally, they hardly ever express regret or acceptance of guilt.

5. Insisting that everything must revolve around them. When you try to discuss the challenges you've been facing, people may change the subject and become defensive or angry. These actions point to narcissism. At its root, narcissistic behavior results from the failure to listen. Imagine it as one-sided hearing when the other person dismisses what you have to say and may become agitated quickly if your point of view differs from theirs.

Additionally, most of the decisions narcissists make are influenced by their emotions. They don't even think about how buying a new sports car would affect the family finances; they have to have one because they want one.

When people feel bored or unhappy, they go to the outside world for a change of pace. For example, they might end or start a new relationship, move across the country, change their employment, or launch a new business. They constantly look to something or someone outside of themselves to meet their wants and satisfy their feelings. Additionally, they want you to support their preferences and decisions because otherwise, they would become irritated and resentful not to mention abusive.

6. Constantly feeling the desire to be noticed. Narcissists require ongoing care. A narcissist will never believe you, no matter how often you tell them they are loved, admired, or approved. They are insecure and worry that they won't measure up to support a wounded ego, part of their persistent desire for affirmation and approval from others.

7. The inability to be genuinely vulnerable. Narcissists share the inability to fathom emotions and feel empathy. They have a constant need for self-protection that renders them incapable of loving or emotionally connecting with others. They are unable to view the world from the viewpoint of another person. They frequently overlap relationships or begin a new one as soon as feasible when one connection is no longer fulfilling.

8. Personalizing any criticism. Avoid attempting to reason with a narcissist in the hopes that they will comprehend how their actions affect you. While narcissists may claim to understand your sentiments, they genuinely do not. You may erroneously believe they will change their conduct if they know how their actions have harmed you.

The narcissist reduces, negates, ignores, and dismisses the worries and views of others. When anything goes wrong, narcissists tend to place the blame elsewhere and become abusive. Finding fault with and putting the blame on others feels safer than trying to understand and develop from challenges.

An important sign of narcissism is how a person listens. Someone who seeks to comprehend others is likely to be emotionally stable. Neglecting or dismissing the opinions of others implies narcissistic tendencies. Narcissism generally is not a set characteristic like height or eye color, although some people are more prone to the condition than others. Narcissism, on the other hand, frequently resembles a lack of listening abilities.

If you identify with any of these descriptions, then try to improve your listening and decision-making abilities. You might be surprised that as your relationships become more substantial and satisfying, there is less conflict. Abuse is swept away in the process.

Key Findings

- A person who is extraordinarily sensitive to the emotions of those around them is known as an empath. Empaths have a unique perspective on the world because they have a deep awareness of others. Not all empaths are necessarily HSPs, but there may be a distinction between the two. Empaths are susceptible to the "feel" or environment of their surroundings. They thrive in environments of tranquility and peace because they internalize those attributes.
- Empaths also have a propensity for attentive listening and will wait patiently for someone to finish speaking before responding emotionally. You can sense other people's emotions and bodily ailments as an empath. This includes experiencing physical discomfort in the same bodily regions, such as pain, tightness, or soreness. Empaths are drawn to professions like nursing, medicine, caring for the elderly, or healing. It's practically impossible for someone to conceal their genuine intentions because empaths can read even the most minor social clues.
- People seek out empaths for assistance but feel better at ease in their company. Empaths are considerate and sensitive, ensuring every team member feels heard. Narcissists are not. A licensed mental health professional can only diagnose narcissistic personality disorder (NPD). There are no precise scientific methods, blood tests, or X-rays to determine whether someone has NPD. Narcissists typically lack empathy for others and tend to be selfish, self-absorbed, and abusive.

3

DISTINCTIVE EMPATH TRAITS

Empathic persons are quite the opposite of narcissists. they tend to have highly charming personalities and a remarkable capacity to attract others to them. They are individuals who can read a room and your thoughts. Of course, not literally, but they can detect your body's signals and infer your mood. An empathic individual can see through any attempts you make to conceal who you are.

Empaths have some highly distinctive personality traits that other people don't have. Being an empath might be challenging, but they also traits that are advantageous to others.

Let's look at it, so you will know what to expect the next time you run into this type of individual.

1.) They're Quite Sensitive. Empathic people are exceedingly sensitive. Not only are they emotionally sensitive, but they are also keen on specific sounds, lighting, environments, and people. It might be exhausting for them to be in particular locations with specific individuals at specific times since they absorb all of the energy presents there. They soak up everything around them like sponges.

Psychotherapist Lisa Hutchison, LMHC, claims that empaths "are like sponges that absorb the thoughts, feelings, and sensations surrounding them. You might find that you feel depressed after chatting to someone who is depressed,"

An empath, however, also has a strong sense of empathy and can support individuals around them since they can relate to their struggles. An empath's capacity for empathy is often exaggerated, leading to the belief that they can intuitively know the wants, sensitivities, tastes, and even thought patterns of those near them.

2) They Don't Hide How They Feel. While there are many things that empaths excel at, one of them is not hiding their emotions and sentiments from others. That's a good thing. With an empath, you'll always know what you're receiving and where you stand. In *Psychology Today*, M.D., Judith Orloff writes that "empaths view the world through intuition. They must cultivate their intuition and pay attention to their feelings about individuals. They express their emotions honestly and openly without worrying about what other people would think when they act on their gut instinct. They work hard at loving, living, and having fun before collapsing from tiredness at the end of the day. There is no doubt about their feelings because they are so transparent.

3) They Always Avoid Crowded Areas. It might be challenging for empaths to be in a crowded place or at a party because they absorb so much energy from other people. They might even find it challenging to find employment with major companies that have hundreds of employees. Because their attention is frequently directed outward rather than inside, empaths are easily triggered by noise, according to Lisa Hutchison.

To help others, empathic people feel obligated to listen and interact with them, yet doing so also depletes their energy. It's intriguing to consider how someone who genuinely cares about other people may get exhausted by their acts of giving and listening.

4) They find the source of their joy

An empath will spend a lot of time alone trying to understand the source of their negative or depressing feelings. They typically prefer one-on-one or small group interactions and tend to be introverted, according to Judith Orloff. Even if they are more extroverted, empaths might choose to spend less time socializing or in large crowds.

They take responsibility for their irrational emotions rather than blaming others for how they feel. They have enough self-awareness to realize that it takes a little time to work on problems before they can get back on the horse. They become happier persons by taking time for themselves and healing their hearts.

5) Those Emotions Won't Go Away. If you know an empath, you've probably already discovered that they can't control their feelings for very long. They recognize that their inner experiences shape who they are. According to psychic and spiritual counselor Davida Rappaport's analysis for *Bustle*, a sure sign of an emotional personality is a propensity to cry at the slightest provocation. However, you might also be an empath.

Empaths are aware that being around too many or diverse kinds of people can make them tired, but they are also aware that other people may find their traits draining. They are perfectly content with how they are, thank you.

6) They Offer Excellent Counsel. If you ever get the chance, seek an empath's counsel and follow their guidance. They can put themselves in your shoes and give you advice on what they would do since they are such good listeners and because they absorb talks. According to

Davida Rappaport, "you might realize that you're in sync with some folks from time to time." Saying phrases like "I had the same idea or emotion" or "It's as if you read my mind or something" to another person regularly indicates a psychic connection between you.

They can conjure feelings to accompany their bodily visualization of accomplishing such activities. Aside from getting quality time with an empath, you may also leave with some truly excellent solutions to your difficulties.

7) They Have a High Propensity Towards Distraction. Despite how concentrated they are in life, empaths are easily distracted, which is one of the strange things about them. They observe the shining, dazzling aspects of life and its shadowy side. You may find that you have a lot of emotions and feelings rushing around, as psychic and spiritual counselor Davida Rappaport believes.

They can make time for another project of comparable importance if working on one that is already significant to them. Empaths understand that such items drew their attention for a purpose and must be attended to, whereas many people would crumble under such a squirrelly personality feature.

They cherish something about themselves because one of their distinctive personality quirks makes them who they are. Nothing is overlooked, and nothing is abandoned.

8) They Require Solitude. There is no avoiding it. Empaths must have enough alone time to refuel their energies and senses. In actuality, even a short period of solitude can prevent emotional overload. An empath might quickly feel depleted and worn out if they don't get enough alone time. Empaths do this because they take on other people's energy, and they experience emotions shared by others. Taking on others' abuse is the most exhausting of all.

Empaths require their alone time even when they are in a close relationship. When empaths don't have time to "decompress" in their own space, according to Judith Orloff. They tend to absorb their partner's energy and get overwhelmed, nervous, or weary.

This is a typical reason why empaths stay away from relationships because they secretly fear becoming consumed. Judith advises empaths to start new love relationships to assert their desire for personal space. It will be easier for an empath to achieve complete emotional liberation by setting aside time alone.

9) Empaths may be easy prey for energy vampires. An empath is sensitive, empathic, and caring while narcissists may find them easy prey because of these qualities. The main issue is the strong attraction between empaths. Right, opposites do attract. On the other hand, empaths have the propensity to overlook everything a narcissist does, so the two are a poor match.

A narcissist uses the sensitive quality of an empath to satisfy their ongoing want for praise and attention because they crave the acceptance of their inherent superiority. An empath may get emotionally exhausted due to a narcissist's total lack of empathy, and their self-esteem may also be destroyed.

For this reason, Aletheia Luna, an expert on empaths, advises empaths to spend time with emotionally intelligent individuals rather than energy vampires. One of the plain sailing ways to determine if someone is compatible with you is to measure their emotional intelligence. Do they have compassion and empathy? Will they be considerate of your sensibilities? Or do they have emotional disabilities? Keep in mind that we frequently draw selfish, unempathetic people.

10) An empath may have trouble with boundaries. An empath's kind nature causes them always to seek the approval of others. They dread disappointing others since they are susceptible to their feelings. It can be challenging for an empath to say "no" when a coworker asks for assistance or when a friend requests to schedule a catch-up.

They have an amiable disposition. This is why a narcissist or a manipulator can exploit an empath's empathy.

An empath needs to master the art of saying "no." After all, defending your own needs for privacy and self-defense is not impolite. If empaths can understand that "no" is a complete statement and you don't need to enter into an extended conversation about the fact that you're saying no, they can avoid many heartaches, as *Business Insider* recommends.

11) **Empaths have a keen sense of intuition.** Blaise Pascall said, "dull minds are never either intuitive or mathematical," And Einstein said, "the only valuable thing is intuition." Why does this matter? It implies that intuition is a very desirable quality. If you're an empath, your intuition probably comes in buckets. What is intuition precisely, and why are empaths so sensitive to it?

Gut feelings are the beginning of intuition. Usually, when a choice needs to be made, it grows from there. Because you're incredibly sensitive to your feelings and those of others, you may instantly recognize that gut sensation if you're an empath. And because you have such a strong understanding of your feelings, you immediately put your faith in them. As a result, trusting your gut instincts while making choices is considerably less of a hassle.

For instance, perhaps you instantly judge someone based on their facial expression and decide not to trust them. Or maybe you can sense when someone is acting "odd" when you're engaging with them.

On their website, *Psychology Today* stated that "intuition is a mental matching game. The brain quickly scans its memory banks after taking in a circumstance to identify the closest analog in the vast array of memories and information it has stored. You can then follow your intuition and take appropriate action."

Not many people are so fortunate. Either they cannot comprehend what their intuition is trying to tell them, or they lack the confidence to believe it. It's crucial to recognize that even if empaths have great intuition, that doesn't imply they always pay attention to or even comprehend it. When an empath has mastered those abilities, according to psychology theory, they are said to be "very intuitive empaths." If not, they can be subject to abuse as ready targets.

Two fast indicators of a very intuitive empath are listed below:

1. You can distinguish between your own emotions and those of other people: Empaths can distinguish between their feelings and those they have absorbed from people around them because they are so tuned in to their inner selves.

2. You can look past emotions to the causes behind them: While empaths are adept at recognizing feelings and emotions, it can be challenging to comprehend why someone is feeling a certain way. Empath tends to get increasingly better at understanding the reasons behind their feelings as they mature, expand, and come to know themselves. In other words, intuitive empaths notice things that conventional empaths miss. They typically comprehend why they or those around them are feeling a certain way.

12) **Empaths must go to bed by themselves.** Do you sleep more soundly on your own? If so, you may be an empath. According to Judith Orloff, sleeping next to another person could feel nearly impossible for an empath. This is because empaths are susceptible to the emotional states of others and find it difficult to turn off their skills when another person is close by. This is especially true if the individual sitting next to them is distressed or emotionally charged.

As empath specialist Lilyana Morales puts it, "mirroring another person's sensations or being aware (hypervigilant) could give a sense of safety or feeling more in control." Unfortunately, empaths' hypervigilance can keep them up even if they know the need for sleep.

. . .

13) A city is not as peaceful for an empath as nature is. An empath can become easily overwhelmed in a city, while most people in major cities become motivated by being near others. Because they are conscious of the strain everyone is under, they act accordingly. And in a vast metropolis, tension is prevalent everywhere.

An empath may spend the entire day in the city before returning home feeling exhausted. They might not even be aware that they are absorbing other people's energy all day. An empath tends to avoid crowds because of this. However, an empath gains vitality in nature's wonder, silence, and beauty, restoring their senses and giving them a sense of energy.

An empath can learn a lot from folks who live in rural areas because they are typically more laid-back and easygoing than city dwellers. Because of this, empaths prefer to be among laid-back individuals who aren't there for any particular reason (many opportunists can be found in a metropolis). They prefer to hang out with unhurried, sincere, and quiet folks. They may be subconsciously shunning abuse.

14) Empaths frequently identify as introverts. Empaths frequently identify as introverts since social situations can quickly deplete them. An extrovert generally gains energy around others, while an introvert loses theirs. Research has proven that introverts have a higher sensitivity to dopamine. This chemical frequently fires in the brain when people are engaged in a protracted social setting.

A moment alone is necessary for an empath to restore their emotional sensitivity. Although an empath may appear unpleasant or unsociable at times, they are only attempting to conserve their energy. Therefore, if you ask an empath to hang out, know that they don't mean it, and when you see them again, they'll be more refueled than before.

Expert on empaths, Donna G. Bourgeois, discusses why empaths should be cautious about expending too much energy on others: "Empaths must be careful to avoid internalizing other people's emotions, as doing so might make them feel uneasy, depressed, or even melancholy. The empath could experience fatigue or drain after that. Toxic people must not be allowed to drain themselves dry; thus, they must learn to create boundaries."

15) Empaths are very wise.
Empaths typically watch more and speak less since they take in more than they give. Before forming an opinion or passing judgment, they tend to engage all their senses in the environment. They are less susceptible to being persuaded by popular opinion because they like to take a step back and study everything around them.

In the end, you can be sure it has not been done so hastily when an empath makes a strong claim or draws a judgment. They have used their senses to take in their surroundings and thoroughly analyze the scenario. For this reason, having an empath on your team or in your corner can be helpful.

The best quote on the topic is from Anthon St. Maarten: "Never underestimate the empowered empath. Even though we are fearless champions for truth and justice and finely calibrated human lie detectors, our warmth and compassion are frequently misunderstood for weakness or inexperience."

16) They enjoy learning about others and listening to what they say. The spark that ignites an empath's passion is learning. When they find out about someone else, they feel they are stepping into a brand-new, intricately gorgeous world. Due to the other person's perception that they are the only person in the world at the time, empaths are excellent conversationalists.

Others feel at ease and comfortable right away as a result. They are aware that egos dominate far too many interactions. But when an empath is present, egos are left outside the door. No wonder empaths are abusive.

. . .

17) They value life's experiences more than material possessions. It might be challenging to meet the needs of one's profound soul, such as those of an empath. Empaths don't enjoy material goods much, but walking in the woods helps them feel healthy and alive. Deeply spiritual individuals must search beyond their possessions for solace and a renewed sense of life. An empath won't achieve this with just a new cell phone. A deep soul requires nonmaterial things to thrive, which is why an empath wants to spend their free time learning, being outdoors, and enjoying experiences with the people they love.

Prioritizing oneself

What is your current top priority? Is it to purchase the car you have been saving for? On the side business, will you be enable to quit your 9-to-5 job one day? Eventually will you ask your partner to move in and take the risk? There is a hidden trap in how you set your goals, no matter what they are.

This is the trap: only when your values and ambitions align can you truly feel satisfied with your life because the journey is much more enjoyable when ideals and objectives are in line, significantly increasing your chances of success. Consider career coach Jeanette Brown's free values exercise on line if you struggle to express your most profound life values. It only takes a few minutes and will provide insightful information on your core principles.

13 Empath Indicators

If you hear the word "empath", you may assume, "Oh, you can read minds?" And you would be pretty close. Empaths are acutely aware of what those around them are feeling, even though the trait isn't quite telepathic as seen in the movies. Judith Orloff's *The Empath's Survival Guide* lists thirteen indicators that you are an empath before you declare yourself the Phoebe Halliwell of your peer group.

According to Psychology Today, an empath has the intrinsic ability to feel and understand the thoughts, feelings, and bodily sensations of others and react to them as if they were their own, frequently without explicit verbalization. Even the most sensitive empaths, when overcome with emotion, have been known to have panic attacks, sadness, chronic exhaustion, or binge eating.

13 Indicators that You're Empathetic

1. People say you are moody.

Most likely you are an emotional sponges. One of the main empath traits is the propensity to pick up on others' energy. So even though you are an emotional person, you might be gloomy due to absorbing everyone's energy, not to mention abuse, subtle or obvious.

2. Among your friends and family, you have a reputation for being the "peacemaker."

You will exert all your effort to maintain calm since negative energy drains you, mainly because it causes conflict in your social or familial circle. Additionally, you're a terrific mediator because you have a good sense of other people's emotions. If emotions go out of control, you can still present the facts without passing judgment and bring things back on course.

3. You don't like crowded, loud, or large public settings

If you need to learn how to prevent the emotions of all those mall rats from seeping into your psyche, you will find that locations like malls or theme parks are unusually draining. After spending time in crowded areas, you'll also want a lot of downtime to center on yourself and recover.

4. When someone yells at you or becomes furious with you, you feel physically sick.

If you're easily overwhelmed, this level of directness may be too much. Instead of engaging in a yelling match, you're more comfortable working things out over a cup of tea and truly getting to the bottom of the problem.

5. You find it intolerable to watch acts of cruelty or violence on TV.

If you could not support the current real crime despite your best efforts, you might be an empath if Sarah McLachlan moved you to cry and contribute to pet rescue programs.

6. People are prone to blame you for their difficulties.

Empaths are renowned for having excellent, sensitive listening skills. Your pals are continually phoning you with any problem, no matter how tiny. Combine that with your propensity to suck up other people's emotions and difficulty in saying "no."

7. Your intuition is really powerful.

You have a sixth sense and often know things without being told. Therefore, while making decisions, you follow your instinct since every time you've disregarded it, it has caused regret.

8. You experience extreme unease with "false" persons

Again, being around "fake" and inauthentic individuals might give you the impression that they are concealing something, which makes you uncomfortable. As a result of having an innate grasp of concepts even before you can articulate them, this may be the case.

9. You're intrigued by alternative healing modalities

Reiki? Acupuncture? Tapping? You'll play. The possible explanation: You sense a metaphysical presence that you're attempting to unravel and comprehend. There is a purpose to the way in which

Sara McLachlan's advertisement makes you feel. According to many empaths, being outside or around animals is incredibly grounding, especially when there isn't any energy from toxic people or energy vampires to distract you.

11. You require solitude.

If you want to feel like yourself again, you need time alone, whether in the great outdoors or bed watching reruns of Schitt's Creek, Friends, or Seinfeld.

12. You believe you don't belong there

Even if you're constantly flooded with feelings, it might be challenging to explain to others why some events strongly affect you, especially if they don't understand what an empath is. Additionally, it can be challenging to fit in if you don't enjoy doing what everyone else does. Some people prefer to attend high-energy activities like concerts, sporting events, and the like, while others prefer to spend time in a quiet library and read.

13. You have trouble drawing boundaries.

Setting limits and being tough can be challenging for empaths, even if it can feel heavy being a loved one's emotional compass. As previously mentioned, these beings find it difficult to say "no," and when they do, they frequently feel guilty.

If you still need more information, consult a mental health expert.

Key Findings

- Empathic persons tend to have highly charming personalities and a remarkable capacity to attract others to them. They soak up everything around them like sponges. Empaths believe they can intuitively know the wants, sensitivities, tastes, and even thought patterns of those near them. Empaths are aware that being around too many or diverse kinds of people can make them tired. They take responsibility for their irrational emotions rather than blaming others for how they are feeling.
- An empath will spend a lot of time alone trying to understand the source of their negative feelings. Empaths can conjure feelings to accompany their bodily visualization of accomplishing tasks. Empaths require alone time even when in a close relationship. When empaths don't have time to "decompress" in their own space, they absorb their partner's energy. An empath is sensitive, empathic, and caring; narcissists may find them easy prey for abuse.
- Expert advises empaths to spend time with emotionally intelligent individuals rather than energy vampires. Empaths have the propensity to overlook everything a narcissist does, so they are a poor match. Empaths are susceptible to their own emotions as well as the emotions of those around them. They are said to be very intuitive, which means they have a strong understanding of their feelings and can follow their gut instincts immediately when faced with a choice. Empath tends to get increasingly better at understanding the reasons behind their feelings as they mature, expand, and come to know themselves. Empaths are susceptible to the emotional states of others and find it difficult to turn off their skills when another person is close by.

4

SEVEN EMPATH TYPES YOU SHOULD KNOW

Recognizing your inner empath.
You might be an empath if you have an intense world experience. As noted, empaths are susceptible to the moods, ideas, and experiences of those around them. In short, they have a keen awareness of people, groups, and physical spaces.

Being an empath means being strong, but because empaths tend to soak up outside emotions like a sponge, life can often feel too much. According to Greatist, there are up to 14 different categories of empaths. Telepathic, emotional, psychometric, molecular, indigo, dream, and other types of empaths are among them. While some may have several traits, other empaths may be more skilled in just one.

You may be an empath. Here is a list of seven empathetic characteristics. Accept your unique abilities to improve the world if you can correlate with one or more.

Emotional Empath

This kind of empath experiences other people's emotions. According to mindbodygreen, this form of empath is the most prevalent.

Emotional empaths both pick up on and adopt other people's emotions. If they can't set limits, life could feel like a roller coaster as they absorb both pleasant and bad feelings not to mention abuse.

Physical Empath

The physical empath can sense how other people's bodies are doing. According to Greatist, if someone gets a stomach ailment, the physical empath will likewise experience that agony in their own body. The physical empath may also mimic people's bodily tics and mannerisms. This power is likened to unintentionally yawning after another person starts to yawn since they do it so effortlessly and without thinking!

Intuitive Empath

According to the spiritual database, a clairvoyant is another term for an intuitive empath. The intuitive empath may learn about someone's life, past, blockages, and behaviors just by looking at them. They are also capable of deciphering spoken undertones.

Plant Empath

Plant empath adores plants, senses their needs, and can even "hear" their thoughts. They appreciate being surrounded by houseplants and have an intense interest in gardening. According to Well+Good, a plant empath or parent will wither along with its flowers. Because they are concerned for everyone, they are terrific buddies.

Animal Empath

An animal empath is deeply connected to all animals and can intuitively perceive a pet's needs. Are you searching for signs of animal empathy? They might be interested in dog and cat rescue and have a house full of animals.

Solancha asserts that the animal empath can converse with animals and comprehend their moods. They frequently reject wearing leather and are vegans. When animals are abused, people will experience intense sadness. On the other side of the coin, animals are drawn to them because they can sense the compassion and sensitivity of animal empaths.

Empath Earth

According to mindbodygreen, earth empaths love Mother Nature and are frequently impacted by the weather, especially during a natural disaster. These empaths, also known as geomantic, often sense the accumulated energy of a place or city. The Earth Empath might advocate for environmental conservation before coming home to a house filled with earth tones, plants, and stones.

Heyoka Empath

According to Greatist, this form of empath is the rarest and most intriguing. Heyoka means spiritual fool or sacred clown in the Dakota and Lakota languages of Native America. These empaths are the most potent, as their empathic ability enables them to aid in the development of others.

When with a person who needs support with their spiritual development, the heyoka will truly mirror them. This enables individuals to perceive themselves accurately and prompts them to reconsider their ideals.

Key Findings

- According to Greatist, there are up to 14 different categories of empaths. While some may have several traits, other empaths may be more skilled in just one

- Emotional empaths both pick up on and adopt other people's emotions.
- The physical empath can sense how other people's bodies are doing.
- The intuitive empath may learn about someone's life, past, blockages, and behaviors just by looking at them.
- Plant empath adores plants, senses their needs, and can even "hear" their thoughts.
- An animal empath is deeply connected to all animals and can intuitively perceive a pet's needs.
- The Earth Empath might advocate for environmental conservation before coming home to a house filled with earth tones, plants, and stones.
- Heyoka empath is the rarest and most intriguing empath type.

5

SIX EMPATHS: GIFTS AND DIFFICULTIES

You might be curious about your sort of empath if you've noticed any indicators of it within yourself. Since no two empaths are alike, empathy carries many gifts.

Reiterating information from the last chapter, the six most common varieties of empaths are:

- Emotional empaths
- Physical empaths
- Geomantic empaths
- Earth empaths
- Animal empaths
- Intuitive empaths

Let's look at each sort of empath in more depth, including their special gifts, and their difficulties.

1. The Empath with Emotions

People who are emotional empaths are capable of experiencing other people's bodily emotions. In reality, emotional empaths may feel that other people's emotions are contagious.

Researchers discovered that a particular group of brain cells are in charge of the capacity to demonstrate and experience compassion. This can be connected to the mirror neuron system. And empaths seem to have particularly receptive mirror neurons.

They can profoundly comprehend and connect with the sentiments and emotions of others. As a result, an emotional empath can shed a tear alongside a total stranger because they have susceptible mirror neurons that react to the emotions they are experiencing.

What Talents Do Emotional Empaths Possess?

Emotional empaths frequently make great conversation partners because of their highly responsive mirror neurons. Others feel understood and heard because of their capacity to "experience" the emotions of others. As a result, the emotional empath tends to express their inner thoughts with family, friends, coworkers, and occasionally strangers.

Emotional empaths are excellent therapists and counselors because of their unique capacity to empathize with others.

The Difficulties of Being an Emotional Empath

The inability of many emotional empaths to shield their energy fields from other people's emotions is one of the drawbacks of emotional empathy. Thus, they can inadvertently accept abuse. Therefore, they take in all that their brain registers, making them susceptible to feeling exhausted.

Additionally, emotional empathy can make it challenging to differentiate between your own emotions and those of others. As a result, emotional empaths may struggle to operate normally and feel perplexed about why they feel the way they do.

How to Manage Being an Emotional Empathetic Person

Recognizing your emotional empathy abilities and making the greatest use of them is critical. Additionally, it's important to be aware of the energy you let in because emotional overload is a common problem for empaths. You may be a content empath by learning to guard your energy field and let go of daily stress.

2. The Physical Empath

Physical empaths experience and take on other people's suffering and symptoms. You might be a physical empath if you frequently become sick when near someone who is battling a particular illness.

According to Dr. Judith Orloff, many physical empaths cannot shut out things like others. They frequently experience illness and are diagnosed with panic disorders, pain, persistent depression, exhaustion, and other conditions.

What Talents do Physical Empaths Possess?

Although having a physical empath may feel like a hardship, it is a wonderful gift. Physical empaths can excel as outstanding medical professionals due to their capacity to feel other people's suffering. Their capacity for empathy makes it easier to identify the cause of suffering and support others as they recover. They can affect many lives when the physical empath is under their control.

The Obstacles Facing a Physical Empath

Being a physical empath can be very draining and painful when you aren't adequately safeguarded, even though it can be a fantastic ability when you work in the medical or therapeutic profession. Some physical empaths are bedridden or have long-term illnesses.

Additionally, they fear stepping outside because it exhausts them and interferes with their ability to function due to other people's tension, rage, and pain. For physical empaths, this highlights the significance of self-care and anchoring.

How to Manage Your Physical Empathy

One must establish a daily self-care practice to thrive as a physical empath. Before going to bed at night, cleanse your energy field and protect it in the morning. Even between clients, if you are a health practitioner, you might want to cleanse your energy field.

Many of these symptoms will disappear as you learn to center yourself, safeguard your energy field, develop healthy boundaries, and let go of sorrow from the past and other people.

3. Geomantic Empaths

Have you ever been content without understanding why at a particular location? You may have geomantic empathic abilities! Empaths with a keen sense of the physical environment are geomantic empaths—physical landscapes, such as a location or particular setting.

Additionally, with no apparent reason, some empaths experience various emotions at specific locations, like happiness, recharging, or extreme discomfort. Furthermore, geomantic empaths strongly connect to particular places and are drawn to holy sites, churches, and other spiritual settings.

What Talents do Geomantic Empaths Possess?

Geomantic Empaths are experts at deciphering a location's past. They could pick up on energy associated with specific areas or occurrences. As a result, individuals may feel fear, excitement, pain, or other feelings associated with a particular place.

This talent frequently arouses a strong desire to learn more about particular locations and their histories. Thus, geomantic empaths flourish in fields like history and archaeology.

The Obstacles Facing a Geomantic Empath

This type of empath has drawbacks, including possibly finding it difficult to recognize when nature or a particular location is harmed. They might even start crying as a result. They have such a deep sense of place that they value being destroyed when they witness a location; it hurts them.

In addition, it might be difficult for these kinds of empaths to comprehend why a particular environment elicits such powerful feelings. Geomantic empaths may also become perplexed about their feelings due to the constant shifting of settings and emotions.

Anxiety and in the worst circumstances, depression could arise. Geomantic empaths must maintain their grounding and connection to the soil to deal with these emotions. They can think about getting a grounding mat that they can use all year long.

Another difficulty for this kind of empath may be that some areas or things overwhelm them. As a result, many geomantic choose to exclude them from particular locations.

How to Manage Your Geomantic Empathy

The geomantic empath must put a lot of effort into grounding their energy, as described. So, consider including a grounding practice in your daily schedule. For instance, picture yourself "anchoring" your energy in the earth's core the first thing in the morning. Then imagine how any energy that doesn't belong to or serve you are sent through this thread and recycled in the earth. You can feel everything you need to feel by doing this, but you won't have to hold it inside of you for too long.

4. Earth Empaths

Earth empaths have a strong connection to the planet and all of its inherent forces. These empaths can be energized by strong waterfalls, beams of sunlight, and moonlight. Additionally, earth empaths can detect changes to the planet, such as variations in the weather, astrological shifts, or ocean tides. Earth empaths frequently announce that it is time for everyone to go indoors because it is about to rain. Relatable?

What Talents do Earth Empaths Possess?

Earth empaths have a special bond with nature because of their excellent tuning with the earth. They are the protectors of mother earth, ensuring that she is treated honorably and responsibly. Because of their strong bond with the planet, earth empaths are outstanding campaigners. They will stop at nothing to prevent anyone from endangering our environment.

Problems With Being an Earth Empath

Being an earth empath is a fantastic ability, but experiencing all the energies of the earth can be difficult. This can be highly upsetting, mainly when something negative is happening. For instance, earth empaths can sense an earthquake or tsunami coming and become quite disturbed.

Some earth empaths may also suffer from SAD since they are susceptible to weather and daylight fluctuations (SAD).

How Should I Manage my Earth Empathy?

Earth empaths require frequent connections to mother earth's energy because of their intense relationship with her. The earth empath easily recognizes this connection through grounding exercises. The process can be aided by using a grounding mat, particularly during the chilly winter.

Earth empaths should also concentrate on doing things that benefit the environment. When you walk outside, take a bag with you so you may pick up trash along the way. Or you could back a few projects that are beneficial to the condition of our world. The earth empath will feel more at ease if the planet's needs are met.

5. Intuitive Empaths

A lot of similarities exist between intuitive empaths and emotional empaths. They can tell the difference between their feelings and those of other people. They can identify which emotions, moods, or pains originate from their surroundings because they are tuned in to their internal condition. As a result, they can forge an energetic barrier that allows them to choose to distance themselves from other people.

What Talents Does an Empath Intuitive Possess?

These empaths can see the big picture and connect between cause and effect because they are tuned to their inner condition. As a result, this aids in understanding both their own emotions and the emotions and feelings of others. This ability enables intuitive empaths to assume caregiving jobs such as therapist, coach, or teacher.

Difficulties of Being an Empathic Intuitive

Although intuitive empaths possess a tremendous talent for intuition, they need clarification when they cannot distinguish between their intuition and a sensation. They would be all over the place if they interpreted every emotion as an intuitive cue.

As a result, it might be difficult to tell what is genuinely a gut feeling and what isn't. Additionally, intuitive empaths can tell when someone is lying to them, which can be perplexing because they lack evidence. Can they detect impending abuse?

How Should I Manage My Intuitive Empath Status?

The intuitive empath must always make sure their energy is grounded. Otherwise, they risk losing track of their own emotions and sensations as they grow overly tied to those of others. Additionally, it is more difficult to connect to your intuition when there is a lot of noise, fear, wrath, or resentment. Daily meditation helps the intuitive empath experience the inner calm required to connect to their intuition.

6. Animal Empaths

Animal empaths can discern the mental state of an animal; and they are thus able to affect the animal's behavior. They can be true animal whisperers because they can read the animals' signals. These empaths frequently practice veganism or vegetarianism, are more attracted to animals than people, and often feel like animals are pulled to them.

What Qualities do Animal Empaths Possess?

Animal empaths make excellent animal caregivers because of their unique capacity to empathize with animals. They appear to comprehend the wants of the animals readily. As a result, animals in need frequently find their way into the compassionate arms of an animal empath. Many animal empaths work as veterinarians, dog groomers, dog walkers, or at animal shelters. Both animals and people adore them!!

Problems With Being an Animal Empath

Although they have a talent, animal empaths often struggle in our meat-eating, animal-cruel world. Animal empaths thus suffer with how society treats animals. As a result, they are deeply hurt whenever they witness animal abuse. As a result, animal empaths frequently attempt to improve the world by becoming activists and raising awareness of this sector.

How Should I Manage my Empathy for Animals?

The finest thing you can do if you are an animal empath is to surround yourself with animals. Connect with animals as often as you can, whether as pets or by volunteering at a nearby animal shelter. To completely embrace your energetic state as an animal empath, you might also want to consider turning vegetarian or vegan. Finally, if you're an animal empath, you can find support groups that aid animals immensely satisfying.

Can you have many empathic types?

Reading this material and identifying with more than one empath is possible. There are numerous ways empathy might manifest itself within you. However, one or two of the categories above may be further advanced in you. To genuinely thrive as an empath, we advise you to try the self-care techniques indicated in this area.

Which Type Are You?

Did you determine which of these categories of empaths you are after reading this section? You may fit into more than one type.

Key Findings

- Emotional empaths are capable of experiencing other people's bodily emotions. They can profoundly comprehend and connect with the sentiments and emotions of others as a result.
- Physical empaths experience and take on other people's suffering and symptoms. Their capacity for empathy makes it easier to identify the cause of suffering and support others as they recover.
- Geomantic empaths have a keen sense of the physical environment—physical landscapes, such as a location or particular setting. They pick up on energy associated with specific areas or occurrences.
- Earth empaths have a strong connection to the planet and all its inherent forces. They can detect changes to the planet, such as variations in the weather, astrological shifts, or ocean tides.
- Intuitive empaths can identify which emotions, moods, or pains originate from their surroundings because they are tuned in to their internal condition. They can see the big picture and connect between cause and effect because they are tuned to their inner condition.
- Animal empaths can discern the mental state of an animal, and they are thus able to affect the animal's behavior effectively.
- To genuinely thrive as an empath, we advise you to try out the self-care techniques indicated in this area.

6

THE SYMPTOMS OF AN ABUSIVE RELATIONSHIP

What is an abusive relationship? Any relationship in which one person negatively exercises power and control over the other is called abusive. Abuse can manifest itself in various ways, including physical contact through words, money, emotions, or other means of power and control.

Even though abusive relationships share many characteristics, each one is likely unique. Additionally, abuse can be challenging for those in violent relationships to recognize. One of the most common features of abusive relationships is the abuser's insistence that their behavior is perfectly normal and in no way harmful, making it hard for the victim to understand their situation. It is particularly hard for an empath.

No type of person is impervious to abuse or incapable of abusing others, and everyone is susceptible to abuse regardless of age, gender, color, or sexual orientation. The perpetrator of abuse bears all of the blame, never the victim.

People who are in abusive relationships may experience a variety of issues as a result of the violence, such as:

- Feelings of isolation
- Embarrassment
- Depression
- Anxiety
- Suicidal feelings
- Addictions
- Injuries
- Financial problems

While every relationship entails conflict, good relationships imply two people who can disagree, argue from their respective perspectives. In abusive relationships, one person attempts to dictate the other's emotions, thoughts, or behavior. Knowing the warning signs can assist you in avoiding or leaving an abusive situation.

Signs of an Abusive Relationship

The core elements are the same, even though every abusive person may use a distinct set of control mechanisms. When two people are in an abusive relationship, one person will use their influence over the other to keep them from doing anything but what the abusive person wants. The following are warning indicators to look for:

Communication Monitoring

Abusers may attempt to keep tabs on your interactions with others. They might request access to read your emails and texts, enter into your devices without authorization, or even set up tracking software to monitor your social interactions. Frequently, they'll use this against you in the future.

Isolation

The victims of abusive partners are frequently isolated as well. The abusive individual may spread false information about you or attempt to persuade you that your loved ones don't adore you. The objective is to remove the support networks that would otherwise enable you to end the relationship.

Financial management

In certain abusive relationships, one partner attempts to take away the other's ability to manage their finances. This is done so that the abused person has a harder time ending the relationship. Your account access may be blocked, your financial position kept a secret, or the abusive individual may attempt to force you to quit your place of employment.

Coercion

Coercion implies forcing you to do things you don't want to do, whether through begging, threats, force, or emotional manipulation. It is a frequent abuse strategy that may work on the weak, such as a sensitive empath who wants to please. This applies to any action the empath doesn't want to engage in, not only sexual behavior. If you try to leave the relationship, abusive persons may use coercion to prevent you from doing so.

Emotional manipulation

Emotional abuse is among the most prevalent forms. It manifests in:

- Disregarding you
- Making fun of you in public
- Giving you the impression that you're crazy
- Making you feel bad for carrying out routine actions

In healthy partnerships, both partners work to improve the other person. In abusive partnerships, one person puts the other down.

Physical violence

The most obvious indicator of an abusive relationship is physical violence. If you are ever hit or wounded in any other manner by your partner, your relationship is probably highly abusive.

How to Handle an Abusive Relationship

Breaking up and leaving an abusive partner is the greatest option for anyone in such a situation. Having a strategy in place is crucial because this could be frightening. Before you depart, plan your route and inform your friends or family that you intend to break up with your partner. If you require assistance finding a place to stay or getting back on your feet, you can also contact nearby resources. Note that the empath struggles the most.

Abusive Behaviors

The batterer may have control over the victim's income, the amount of time spent with friends and family, the people they talk to or receive phone calls from, the places they go, the people they hang out with, the clothes they wear, and other aspects of their daily life. Although a batterer may justify these actions as being concerned about their safety and well-being, the true goal is to have as much control over the victim as possible.

Unrealistic expectations: A batterer may have unrealistic expectations that their partner will fulfill all their needs in the manner they desire. They may also have unrealistic expectations that their partner will resolve issues beyond their control, such as work, social relationships, finances, etc.

A jealous batterer will interrogate the victim about the people they interact with, accuse them of flirting and having affairs, dressing seductively, being suspicious of male or female business acquaintances, search their personal belongings for indications of assignations, etc. The abuser could mistakenly believe their actions show affection for the victim.

Blames others: A batterer may assign blame for his or her issues to others. They might attribute the victim's problems in their environment to them. They won't accept accountability for any regrettable or harmful incidents in their lives.

Utilization of children: A batterer may threaten to hurt or remove the children. Even when the victim is aware that made up allegations of child abuse and neglect are unfounded, they may threaten to report them to the police. They could set unrealistic expectations for children's behavior and discipline them when they fall short of those standards. Spanking a two-year-old child for soaking their underwear is one example.

Threats of violence are expressions of the intent to use physical force, harm, or even death to control the relationship. The victim assumes the batterer can carry out these threats because of prior experience. The batterer may push or apply force to the other person, physically restrict them from leaving, or threaten to hurt or kill them if they do.

Destructive acts: When trying to control their victim, perpetrators of domestic violence may resort to physical violence or threats, such as attacks on property or animals. Frequently, the attacker will make threats against the victim's clothing, the family pet, the walls, or the car. Animal cruelty is a sad consequence. A batterer may kick, toss, beat, or injure the household pet. They may break or strike objects to frighten the victim. In the process, they may damage household belongings, kick doors, punch holes in the walls, or toss domestic items about.

Domestic exploitation: This is when the woman is made to perform unbalanced household chores based only on her gender, including cooking, cleaning, taking care of the kids, and serving her male partner and his friends. The abuser anticipates that the victim invariably a woman, will be completely submissive. For instance, a batterer might believe that women are less intelligent, inferior to males, responsible for performing menial duties, and unable to live a whole life without the partnership.

Economic manipulation: The abuser is entirely in charge of all financial matters affecting the family. Threats are made to the victim's financial security to exert control over them.

Verbal or emotional abuse: This type of abuser's behavior is best described as withdrawing or withholding emotional support or verbally abusing the victim harshly. Sulking, sobbing, retreating into a quiet, leaving, arguing, shouting, and making derogatory remarks are some of the typical behaviors. Batterers may use rude and hurtful language, slur or belittle their spouse, or minimize their successes.

Immigration: Threatening to report the victim to immigration is one way an abuser takes control of a relationship in an immigrant family. In an all-too-common scenario, the abuser helps their spouse immigrate to the United States but then holds the documents, making it impossible for them to flee. No matter where a person lives, migration from one nation to another seems to encourage isolation, promoting domestic violence. An immigrant who has been abused might not realize that they can tell the police their account directly or that a judge will believe them.

Physical battery: Physical battery refers to abusive behavior that involves pushing or throwing the victim into walls, out of windows, or out of moving vehicles. It can also include striking, kicking, spitting, slapping, cutting, stabbing, or shooting. These actions could be committed with the intent to kill the victim.

Sexual manipulation/abuse: Sexual manipulation or abuse can take many forms, including forcing sex on a victim who doesn't want it, coercing sex by threats, physically forcing sex, and violent sexual assault. The victim can be made to engage in prostitution or have sex with a stranger under duress. This abuse involves holding people against their will during sex, simulating helpless sexual fantasies, forcing sex when the partner is sleeping, or demanding sex when the partner is ill or exhausted. The abuser does not appear to care about their partner's preferences and might manipulate compliance by pouting, becoming angry, or making threats.

THE SYMPTOMS OF AN ABUSIVE RELATIONSHIP

Social isolation is the purposeful cutting off of a person from their friends and family, which entails directing their movements, conversations, and actions. Women and men fleeing violence may not have a network of friends and family members to rely on for accommodation because of their guilt over the beatings. The abuser will frequently call the victim to inquire about what they are doing, who they are with, etc., before engaging in isolation. As a result, demands to avoid seeing friends and relatives develop alongside complaints about their shortcomings. Threats of physical danger made to the victim if they leave the house unaccompanied by the abuser are typically made during this period.

Batterers may isolate their victims by cutting off or completely controlling their connection to outside resources and assistance. Labeling them as "trouble-makers," the batterer may limit the victim's relationships with friends and relatives. They might deny the victim access to their car, take away their keys, limit their home phone use, seize their cell phones, open and read their mail, restrict their computer use, read all of their emails, etc. They can stop them from going to work, gatherings outside, or church.

Abuse of spiritual beliefs: Often, the abuser may criticize the victim's religious habits and beliefs. The abuser may make insulting remarks about the victim's deeply held, sacred beliefs, which otherwise give them solace. The abuser may purposefully misunderstand biblical verses and texts to persuade women and men that they must succumb to the batterer's demands without question. This is another kind of abuse.

Stalking: To stalk is to act menacingly or persistently or pursue a target or quarry by tracking them covertly. An abuser employs this predatory conduct to control or intimidate the victim or to track them down and possibly kill them. This behavior is displayed by an abuser who has been told to desist from all contact with the victim, including refraining from calling, returning home, visiting the victim's employment, school, or church, and following the victim in a car or on foot. The victim, the victim's family, or a legal process might make the desist request.

The abuser decides not only to disregard the "no contact" order but use every available means to get in touch with the victim or closely monitor their whereabouts. Other stalking behaviors include breaking into the house when the victim isn't there and leaving a trail of their presence. Threatening voicemails could be left by the stalker. Stalking frequently progresses to the point when the abuser harms or murders the victim. This behavior typically follow the victim's departure from the batterer. Stalking is currently considered a distinct felony in many places, including California.

These actions are intended to terrify and hold the victim captive. When confronted with their actions, a batterer may dispute that they have taken place or accuse the victim of pressuring them into acting negatively. Although statistics show that most batterers are men, women can also commit these crimes.

Understanding the Symptoms of Emotional Abuse

Emotional abuse: what is it?

Many of the apparent indicators of emotional abuse and manipulation may be ones you are already aware of. However, it might be simple to overlook the early, undetectable indicators of abuse while dealing with an abusive scenario. This is particularly important for the target empath.

The goal of emotional abuse is to terrorize, dominate, or isolate the victim. Although no physical violence is involved in this abuse, you or your loved ones may be the target of threats. It is demonstrated through a person's words, deeds, and consistency of these behaviors. Even though abuse may begin gently, it persists.

Abusive behavior does not discriminate based on age or gender. Additionally, abuse does not always take place in the context of romantic partnerships. Your spouse or love partner may be abusing you, but it's also possible that they're your business partner, parent,

THE SYMPTOMS OF AN ABUSIVE RELATIONSHIP

caregiver, or even your adult child. It is often perpetuated by a narcissist.

In any case, you don't deserve the treatment, and you are not at fault. Learn the signs of emotional abuse and what to do if you experience them by reading on.

Embarrassment, dismissal, and criticism

Different strategies may be employed by the person abusing an empath to lower their self-esteem.
Examples:

- Harassment and insulting nicknames. They'll outright call you "dumb," "a loser," or other derogatory term. Perhaps they refer to you in terms of "endearment" that draw attention to the sensitive areas of your personality, such as "my little nail biter" or "my fat pumpkin," and they reject your demands to cease.
- The assassination of characters. The phrase "always" is used. You consistently arrive late, make mistakes, are uncooperative, and so on. They might say these things about you or use them to characterize your actions to others.
- Yelling. It might scare you and make you feel tiny and unimportant to scream, rant, and swear. They may strike out, throw things, or cause property damage even if they never hit you.
- Patronizing. By saying, "I know you try, but this is just beyond the span of your brain," they denigrate you.
- Public humiliation They start arguments, divulge your personal information, or publicly ridicule your flaws.
- Dismissiveness. When you tell someone something significant to you, they respond, "What? Who is interested in that?" The same message can be sent via body

language, such as sighing, shaking your head, eye-rolling, and smirking.
- Joking. If you disagree with something they've said, they immediately respond, "Can't you take a joke? Grow up." You end up feeling stupid and doubting whether you are being overly sensitive. Poor empath!
- Making fun of your appearance. They stop you at the door as you leave. "You're wearing that silly clothing, aren't you? That explains why you can't get a date." Or they keep telling you that you're lucky they picked you because they could have chosen someone far more appealing.
- Undermining your achievements. They dismiss your accomplishments and imply they don't matter, or they take credit for your successes.
- Disregarding your interests. They imply that your favorite pastime is a time waster. "Why keep trying when you'll never be good at the piano?" They really would prefer that you refrain from engaging in activities by yourself.
- Pressing your buttons. When they discover something that irritates or unnerves you, they constantly bring it up despite your wishes for them to cease.

Control and shame

The desire to continue in power and control underlies abusive behavior. A person who is abusing another may try to persuade the person to act in a certain way, frequently by making them feel inferior.

They try to get you to do what they want by:

- Threatening others. They hint that they'll dismiss or report you for being an inadequate parent or openly announce the same. They may use evasive language to

THE SYMPTOMS OF AN ABUSIVE RELATIONSHIP

make you fearful, such as "There's no knowing what I might do."

- Keeping track of your location. Always wanting to know where you are, they demand you answer their calls or texts immediately. They might appear at your employment or educational institution to verify your attendance.
- Cyberspying. They regularly monitor your internet history, emails, texts, and call logs, and either demand your passwords or insist you go password-free.
- Gaslighting. Someone abusing you might dispute that those certain occurrences, discussions, or agreements ever took place. This strategy may make you doubt your recollection and mental and physical wellness.
- Making every choice. This could entail canceling health visits and closing a joint bank account. They might ask you to quit your job and withdraw from school, or they might act on your behalf. They might also tell you how to dress, how much to eat, or even which pals you can hang out with.
- Managing your financial access. They demand money from you and maintain bank accounts in their name. They also demand you maintain all your receipts and give a detailed account of your spending.
- Emotional extortion. Someone may persuade you to do something by acting on your emotions. They could pretend to be the victim, pose tough questions to "test" you, or make you feel guilty.
- Never stop the lectures. No matter how small the mistake, they record all of your mistakes in a protracted monologue when you commit one. They make it plain that they think you are beneath them by listing the many ways you have failed.
- Giving clear but negative instructions. They expect you to do anything they say without question, from "Stop taking

medicine" to "You stay here until you get that client back, or you're fired."
- Expelling emotions frequently. They advise you to postpone your friend's outing or park the automobile in the garage, but you don't. They grow upset and shout aggressively about how rude and unhelpful you are.
- Pretending to be helpless Instead of taking the time to explain something, they claim they cannot do it in the hopes that you will figure it out on your own.
- Unpredictability. They suddenly burst into action for no apparent reason before showing love. Or sometimes, they suddenly go from being cheery to furious and dark without notice, leaving you unsure of what to anticipate.
- Moving away. You can find yourself stranded at a social gathering because your partner or parent leaves abruptly. During a discussion regarding your assignment, a supervisor may leave your questions unanswered.
- Standing in your way. They shut down and stop responding to your communications during an argument or fight.

Denial, blaming, and accusations

Abusers frequently attempt to establish a hierarchy in which they are at the top, and you are at the bottom. Consider the following incidences:

- Jealousy. They accuse you of flirting or infidelity or claim you would spend all of your time with them if you truly loved them.
- Using shame. They might use phrases like "You owe me this" to try to guilt you into doing anything. They often say, "Look at everything I've done for you" to gain favor.
- Unreasonably high hopes. They anticipate that you will carry out their instructions at the appointed time. They

believe you should always prioritize their needs and act according to their standards. They also believe that you should never spend time with your friends or family if there is even a remote possibility that they may require you.
- Accusing and goading. Abusers and manipulators frequently have a knack for upsetting you, especially if you are an empath. However, when you do become upset, they put the responsibility back on you since you are so overly sensitive and incapable.
- Disproving the abuse. They can reject it when you raise concerns about their behavior since they seem baffled by the idea. Even worse, they can claim that you are the one who struggles with control and anger or they only become angry because you are such a tough person.
- Trivializing. They say you overreacted or misunderstood the issue when describing how much they upset you and damaged your feelings.
- Charging you with their issues. They constantly blame you when things go wrong. They might remark that their lives would be wonderful if you were a more devoted child, a better partner, or a better parent.
- Destruction and denial. They might knock your phone over to damage it, "lose" your car keys, or obliterate other priceless items while denying it or claiming it was an accident.

Isolation and neglect of emotions

Usually, a person who is abusing you will try to persuade you to put their wants before your own. They frequently try to isolate you by obstructing your relationships with comforting family members, thereby increasing your reliance on them.

They could employ the following strategies:

- Dehumanizing you. They'll purposely turn their heads away or gaze at something else to minimize your importance when speaking to you.
- Preventing social interaction. You can't plan anything without them coming up with an excuse or begging you not to go.
- Discrediting you. They might imply or state outright that they don't care about your needs, boundaries, or desires.
- Seeking to sever the connection to your family. They will explain why you can't attend family gatherings or tell relatives you don't want to see them. They might later claim that your loved ones don't care about you or believe you have a problem.
- Applying the silent approach. Your efforts to discuss with them in person, by text, or on the phone can be ignored.
- Refusing to show affection. They wouldn't touch you even if they wanted to hold your hand or pat your shoulder. If you insult them or they insist that you do something you don't want to do, they might refuse to have any intimate contact.
- Terminating communication. When you wish to discuss significant issues, they might ignore you, wave you off, or shift the subject.
- Working diligently to sway others against you. They may tell others, including friends, family, and coworkers that you are a liar, have lost touch with reality, or suffered an emotional breakdown.
- Refusing assistance. The world can't stop and wait for your troubles; they might remark or advise you to toughen up and fix it yourself if you need emotional support or assistance with a problem.

THE SYMPTOMS OF AN ABUSIVE RELATIONSHIP

- Interrupting: They may come in your face while you are engaged in an activity and take your phone or other items from your hands to make you aware that you should be focusing on them instead.
- Contesting your emotions. They could say that you shouldn't feel that way no matter what emotion or feeling you convey. For instance, "What have you got to be unhappy about?" or "You shouldn't be furious over that."

How to handle emotional assault

Trust your gut if you think you're being emotionally abused. Some starting points:

- Avoid attempting to fix them. You might want to intervene, but it can be challenging for abusive people to alter their behavior without expert assistance. You can suggest that they work with a therapist, but ultimately it is up to them to decide. This is hard for the helpful empath but is a must.
- Keep self-blame at bay. No matter what you've done or said, keep in mind that you never deserve to be abused. The abuser is the only one who must answer for their actions.
- Set your needs as a priority. You can advance to a point where you feel safe setting boundaries, asking for support, and leaving the abusive environment by taking care of your physical and mental needs.
- Don't interact. Please don't respond to their calls, emails, or text messages. Try to keep a companion with you and keep your talk to necessary subjects if you must work or spend time with them.
- Define your boundaries. Choose a strategy to avoid being manipulated or sucked into a debate. Tell the individual abusing you the limitations and then uphold them. Say

something like, "If you call me names, I'll go home," or "If you start making fun of me in front of others, I'll leave."
- Create a network of allies. Even though it is frightening to discuss your experiences, a supportive therapist and family members go a long way toward helping you acquire the healing support you need.
- End the arrangement or situation. If possible, make it obvious that the relationship is finished and sever all ties.
- Give yourself time to heal. Block their phone number and social media accounts. Ignore any attempts to contact you. Take some time to concentrate on your needs and healing. You might need to reclaim your sense of self, establish new self-care practices, and consult a therapist who can provide recovery advice.

Ending an abusive relationship can be more difficult if you're married, have kids, or share assets. Consulting a lawyer is a wise action if it applies to you. You can create an exit strategy to leave the relationship securely with the assistance of a domestic abuse advocate or mental health specialist.

Key Findings

- Knowing the warning signs can assist an empath in avoiding or leaving an abusive situation. Abuse can manifest itself in various ways, including physical contact through words, money, emotions, or other means of power and control. The perpetrator bears all the blame, never the victim. In abusive relationships, one partner may try to control the other's ability to manage their finances. Leaving an abusive relationship is the greatest option for anyone in such a situation.
- A jealous batterer may interrogate the victim about the people they interact with, accuse them of flirting and

THE SYMPTOMS OF AN ABUSIVE RELATIONSHIP

having affairs with other men or women, be suspicious of male or female business acquaintances, search their personal belongings for indications of assignations, etc. The abuser could mistakenly believe their actions show affection for the victim. Batterers of domestic violence resort to destructive acts to control their victim. Threats are made to the victim's clothing, the family pet, the walls, or the car window. The woman is made to perform unbalanced household chores based only on her gender.

- Sexual manipulation or abuse can take many forms, including forcing sex on a victim who doesn't want it. The victim can be made to conduct prostitution or have sex with a stranger under duress. Social isolation is the purposeful cutting off of a person from their friends and family.
- To stalk is to act menacingly or persistently, to menace, or to pursue a target or quarry by tracking them covertly. Stalking is currently considered a distinct felony in many places, including California.
- Although most batterers are men, women can also commit these crimes. The goal of emotional abuse is to terrorize, dominate, or isolate the victim. Even though abuse may begin gently, it persists. Emotional abuse does not discriminate based on age or gender; it can also occur in a business, family, or professional relationship.
- A person who is abusing you may try to persuade you to act in a certain way, frequently by making you feel inferior. They could try to get you to do what they want by keeping track of your location and demanding that you answer their calls or texts immediately.
- A supervisor may try to control you by acting on your emotions. They could pretend to be the victim, pose tough questions to "test" you, or make you feel guilty for making a mistake. Or they might act for no apparent reason before showing your love. Abusers and manipulators attempt to

establish a hierarchy with them at the top and you at the bottom. They might use phrases like "You owe me this" or "Look at everything I've done for you" to guilt you into doing something.

- An abusive person will try to persuade you to put their wants before your own. They might try to isolate you by obstructing your relationships with family members, thereby increasing your reliance on them. They may destroying your valuables for selfish gain or just to cause you distress. They might ignore you, wave you off, or shift the subject when you wish to discuss significant issues. They may tell others, including friends, that you are a liar, have lost touch with reality, or have suffered an emotional breakdown. Or they might advise you to toughen up and fix it yourself if you need emotional support.
- You can advance to a point where you feel safe setting boundaries, asking for support, and leaving the abusive environment by taking care of your physical and mental needs. Don't interact with them and don't respond to their calls, emails, or text messages.

7

TIPS FOR GETTING OVER NARCISSISTIC ABUSE

You're probably feeling a lot of hurt and bewilderment if you recently exited a toxic relationship with a narcissist. Even if you sincerely believe you weren't at fault, believing this is frequently a different matter. Your emotional anguish may increase as you consider what you might have done differently to stop the abuse or assist your loved one in resolving their issues.

According to Ellen Biros, a therapist in Suwanee, Georgia, who specializes in assisting clients in getting over toxic relationships, toxic relationships have certain parallels to addiction. "The connection is addictive," According to Biros. There is sporadic reinforcement and a lot of shame and guilt surrounding the connection. These factors may affect your ability to recover.

You know the union was unhealthy, and you know they mistreated you. However, your pleasant times and how you felt at first are still stuck in your mind. Your desire for companionship and willingness to do whatever to win their affection and approval may be fueled by these recollections.

Trauma from abuse is often severe and may take some time to heal. The advice provided below can help you recover if you're feeling lost.

Recognize the abuse and accept it

The first step toward recovery from abuse is admitting that you have experienced it, whether at the hands of a friend, family member, or intimate partner. This might be hard for an empath.

In the early phases of recovery, letting go of justifications and defenses for the other person's actions may be difficult. You may be relieved to take on the blame for your conduct if it saves you from admitting that a loved one intentionally caused you harm.

This is typical and easily understood. You can feel protected by denial. For many people, intense familial or romantic love eclipses reality. Accepting that some people care little about hurting others is likewise problematic. Denying what occurred, though, keeps you from dealing with it and moving past it. Additionally, it may prepare you for future pain.

If you know that your loved one has struggled with emotional pain, you could feel sympathetic and wish to extend a second opportunity. Although showing compassion is always appropriate, cruelty is never justified by mental illness. You can always support them in asking for help if you give yourself enough room. Biros advises, "Educate yourself on narcissistic tendencies." It may be simpler to accept your experience if you learn to recognize the strategies frequently employed by narcissists.

Establish clear boundaries for yourself.

Specialists in abuse rehabilitation recommend cutting off contact with an ex as soon as feasible. Their inability to stay in touch is a personal barrier and acts as a limit for you, which could seem difficult at first. It's natural to want to get back in touch after receiving a message or phone contact, especially if the sender has taken responsibility and made amends.

Blocking their contact information (including phone number, email, and social media accounts) will help you resist contacting them. Remember that they might still attempt to contact you in other ways, so having a strategy for handling the possibility might be helpful.

Going without communication, however, is only sometimes an option. They might bring their kids, or they might be relatives you occasionally meet at events. If so, consider your wants and needs. For example, "I deserve to be treated with respect." Then make it a limit: "I'm willing to talk to you, but if you yell, swear, or call me names, I'll leave immediately."

Consider setting up personal boundaries like the following to give oneself the necessary room and separation:

- not disclosing private information (a key step in grey rocking)
- limiting communication to a single channel, such as a dedicated email address.

Prepare for complex emotions. Most breakups result in unpleasant emotions, such as:

- grief and loss
- shock
- anger
- sadness or feelings of depression

Biros says you may suffer these and other forms of emotional distress after quitting a relationship marked by narcissistic abuse. This includes:

- anxiety
- fear
- paranoia
- shame

Post-traumatic stress disorder symptoms can also result from the trauma of a toxic relationship (PTSD). Toxic people can be pretty painful. However, they also have a talent for persuading you to accept their version of reality. So even though you could have suffered severe mental damage, you might still be unsure of your behavior.

For instance, your affection for them can lead you to believe it was your responsibility for how they mistreated you and used you as a tool. Feelings of guilt or disloyalty may arise from ending a dysfunctional familial situation.

These feelings are common human emotions. However, independently working through problems is easier, particularly if you need clarification on manipulating techniques. As you go through these challenging emotions, a therapist can assist.

Get your identity back.

Many narcissists are also perfectionists and have high standards for the behavior of those around them. Everyone who doesn't measure up to these standards is harshly ridiculed or condemned. They tend to prey an easy mark, the empath.

What it might resemble:

- You altered your hair because your ex stated it was "dumb and ugly."
- You stopped playing the piano because your parent used to call you "foolish" for "spending time" on music.
- They can attempt to manage your schedule by preventing you from seeing friends or engaging in alone activities.

You feel you no longer know yourself very well if this manipulation has caused you to change your appearance and sense of style or lose things you once valued. The healing process begins with the individual discovering what they value, how they would want to spend their time, and who they would like to spend it with.

Biros suggests not becoming involved with someone new while you're healing. Keep in mind that you are still in the healing process. Introspection and the subsequent efforts to mend broken bonds within might leave you feeling exposed.

Practice self-compassion

You could be extremely self-critical after you admit that your relationship was abusive. Never forget that no one deserves to be abused and that you are not to blame for the other person's conduct. Offer yourself forgiveness instead of blaming yourself for succumbing to their deception or condemning yourself for putting up with their mistreatment for so long.

Both the past and their behavior or deeds cannot be changed. Only you can control yourself. However, you can use this power to decide to respect your needs, such as respect, happiness, and healthy love. Thank yourself for deciding to end the relationship, and motivate yourself to follow through on it.

Try repeating a mantra like "I am strong," "I am adored," or "I am brave" when feeling down on yourself.

Be aware that your feelings might linger.

Because you can't manage love, it can be challenging. Even if someone hurts you, loving them is something you can never stop doing. You can still cherish the good times you shared after the relationship ended and long to return to them. But it's crucial to understand that to begin healing, you don't have to stop loving someone. The healing process may be slowed down by waiting for something to occur.

You can still love someone even though staying in a relationship with them threatens your safety. Accepting this truth might occasionally trigger an emotional separation that makes it easier for you to distance yourself from the relationship.

Take care of yourself.

Effective methods of self-care can hasten the healing process considerably. Practicing self-care means attending to one's own psychological and physiological needs.

Examples of self-care measures:

- receiving adequate, restorative sleep
- unwinding when feeling anxious or stressed
- scheduling leisure pursuits and other enjoyable activities
- staying in touch with loved ones
- using coping mechanisms to control upsetting thoughts
- consuming a variety of foods
- continuing to be active

Taking care of your physical requirements might make you feel stronger and better able to deal with emotional turmoil since your mind and body work together to support one another.

Chat with others.

As you recuperate, being open with encouraging friends and family members might make you feel less alone. However, some individuals in your life might only provide a little (if any) assistance.

The people who care about you:

- offer compassion
- validate the anguish you experience
- help divert you or provide company on rough days
- remind you the abuse wasn't your fault

Some family members could side with the abuser. Mutual friends might defend a controlling ex. This may lead to a great deal of hurt and misunderstanding. Setting limits on how much time you spend with these folks can be beneficial while you try to recuperate.

You could, for instance, request that they refrain from bringing up anybody nearby or discussing their thoughts on the matter with you. Limiting your time with them is possible if they don't abide by those restrictions.

Support groups can allow you to speak up about the abuse you've endured. You can tell your story to those working to heal in a support group.

Biros suggests:

- The website Narcissist Abuse Support provides resources and information on narcissistic abuse.
- Lisa A. Romano, a life coach and the author, has YouTube videos about getting out of toxic relationships.
- Queen Being, a safe, discreet, and cost-free support network for victims of narcissistic abuse.
- Meetups for those who have survived narcissism

Obtain expert assistance

Seeing a therapist for individual sessions can significantly improve mental health. A therapist can help you understand the causes of your reluctance to leave the abuser or your ideas of giving them another chance. They can help you develop a strategy to prevent making unwise decisions in the future. They will no doubt know about empaths' needs.

A therapist can also provide advice on the following:

- acquiring new coping mechanisms
- informing others of the abuse
- resisting the impulse to speak with the abusive person

- coping with symptoms related to mental health, such as depression, anxiety, or others
- overcoming suicidal or self-destructive impulses.

According to Biros, counseling can also assist you in comprehending the underlying causes that might make you more susceptible to abusive practices.

In conclusion, therapy provides a secure environment where a skilled, caring professional can assist you in exploring and comprehending the complex range of feelings you're finding difficult to sort through. Even if it might not happen immediately away, you can heal. As you start the trip, a therapist might make you feel more supported.

Key Findings

- Establish clear boundaries for yourself.
- Be aware that your feelings might linger.
- Take care of yourself.
- Some members of the family could side with the abuser.
- You can tell your story to those working to heal in a support group.

8

HOW TO DEAL WITH ABUSE: A GUIDE (PHYSICAL, EMOTIONAL, OR VERBAL)

Abuse of any kind, whether it be mental, sexual, or physical, can have serious psychological consequences. Consequently, the moment you realize that the relationship you are in is abusive, there are several options for handling it.

The Best Ways to Handle Physical Abuse

Physical abuse is among the hardest things to put up with. Nobody would want to submit to physical assault, which could endanger their life. Here are some strategies for handling physical abuse and avoiding harm.

1. Examine your mental health

The victim of physical abuse may experience severe trauma, and psychiatric disease is typically present in the background. It's crucial to evaluate a physical abuser's mental health and seek undiagnosed mental disorders since they can turn violent and endanger your life. Doing so will prevent things from being ugly and devastating.

Suppose you plan on staying with your abuser. In that case, you must investigate their family history to rule out the possibility of an inherited mental illness. Psychological support is necessary if a mental disease is causing the person's aggressive behavior. But if their actions are motivated by extreme anger, they will need therapy to change this behavior. Whatever the reason, it's critical to fix it before dealing with the person daily.

2. Obtain outside assistance

Leaving an abusive relationship is difficult, especially if there are children present. Family and friends' support will enable you to evaluate the situation and choose the best action. The finest part of having support is being able to talk to the abusive partner, get them counseling, and counsel them about the consequences and how you suffer as a couple due to their violent behavior.

Such discussions occasionally produce unexpected outcomes and prompt offenders to modify their abusive behavior. The situation will improve if the abusive person's family is on your side, as they can talk to the abuser and encourage him to modify his conduct. It is also a huge relief to know that many people are sympathetic to your situation and eager to assist.

3. Consider seeking counseling

Through counseling, an abusive person may change their conduct and mental state. There would be a significant improvement in the person as soon as the therapy sessions are in place, even though you cannot anticipate an immediate transformation. Before you take the drastic measure of ending your relationship with a physically abusive person, explore counseling as a possible relationship-saving measure.

Numerous psychiatric issues that may be simple to treat with counseling or are deeply ingrained can be discovered. For the benefit of your family and kids, give the process ample time to determine if there has been a positive change in the person. Counselors could also recommend a feasible plan of action to follow. Due to their experience, they can forecast whether or not a person can be changed with a high degree of accuracy.

4. Keep yourself safe from harm

Because they lack common sense and act without considering the consequences, abusive persons have the potential to turn violent and pose a serious threat to others. Sharing a house with an abusive individual puts you and your children in danger, so keeping you and them safe is crucial. Avoid aggravating or disturbing the abusive individual in any way, especially if you are alone, late at night, and unable to contact for assistance.

Ensure your children are safe before responding violently if the physically abusive person attacks. Make sure you are not in the person's direct line of sight so they can hurt you physically by locking them up in a secure space. Call for emergency assistance as you defend yourself, ensuring that there are barriers between you and the abusive individual and enough space to leave. It is usually a good idea to let someone know they are expected to recognize danger immediately if you give them a missed or blank call.

5. Walk away

Despite your best efforts and desire for the relationship to succeed, physical violence can sometimes be challenging to treat. Avoid jeopardizing your life by staying with the person in such situations. Either based on mental illness or domestic violence, depending upon which category he falls under. This is crucial for both your security and comfort of mind. Since there is no opportunity for happiness or growth in an abusive relationship, it is in everyone's best interest to take precautions against emotional trauma as soon as possible. The empath must take particular heed and the narcissist gets a warning.

The Best Ways to Handle Emotional Abuse

Ups and downs in relationships serve to emphasize their significance and individuality. However, when one party is gradually undermined, it may be a symptom of emotional abuse. Here are a few strategies for handling emotional abuse.

1. **Write down how the abuser made you feel.** Relationships are essential to life, yet it is unrealistic to expect perfect compatibility. People cannot be changed to suit your needs, and perhaps it is impossible to make the abuser change. However, the most acceptable gestures might convey that you don't support inappropriate behavior.

Let the abuser (the other party) understand their actions are unacceptable. Your feelings are hurt by verbal pain and humiliation, so you do not want to press the issue. Being emotionally abused can render you helpless. Overcome those emotions and develop your confidence to present yourself with assurance. Your self-assurance can make the abuser give up and stop further destroying your self-esteem. Be cautious when defending, though, as many abusers may turn to violent methods if they are met with resistance. The optimum scenario is for the abuser to stop the violence on their own.

When dealing with abuse, exercise emotional intelligence. You can use forums (like a private journal, blog, or small circle of close pals) to express your sentiments, but only within a certain range.

2. **Define the relationship's parameters and restrictions.** Healthy limits must be clearly stated in relationships. If at all feasible, involve the abuser in establishing these boundaries since doing so helps to give the relationship a new dimension. Otherwise, carry out your independent work utilizing reason. Once you have set appropriate limits, you should talk to the abuser about the steps they must take to yield effectively.

Abuse might result from insecurity or a lack of trust. The situation could worsen if you miss or cannot detect abusive behavior. An easy target is a vulnerable and/or empathic victim, such as a youngster subjected to emotional abuse by a parent. In many partnerships, defining boundaries can be challenging and requires expertise. Both sides should accept the principles for reestablishing mutual respect. The person who has been abused should express the limit in explicit terms.

3. Focus your efforts on a positive concept.

It can be unsettling to consider that you are on the receiving end while having done nothing wrong. Conflict might arise as a natural response. Though it frequently does the opposite, it can also work in your favor. Recognize that you have not committed the crime despite being made to feel guilty. Recognize the truth that developing inner strength will improve your endurance.

It's beneficial to talk about the situation with close friends and relatives. They can help to create a cheerful environment where you can consider potential solutions rather than dwelling on the past. Make wise decisions to establish a safe environment. Please make yourself available to reliable friends so that they can assist you when you need it. To distinguish between the good and the unpleasant, follow your intuition.

4. Avoid bad coping mechanisms.

A feeling of helplessness and low self-esteem can result from emotional abuse. Women turn to self-harm as a coping method in these circumstances. You may be less able to handle the issue if you have an eating disorder, a drug addiction, endure physical harm, etc. Keep your feelings to yourself around the abuser. When someone is shouting or screaming, remain calm. Never cave into criticism or threats. Your lack of response and neutral demeanor may discourage the abuser from abusing you more.

Sometimes the abuser will make more effort to injure you (maybe by harming you physically). If you see this propensity, it's best to flee unharmed. Counseling can be helpful when the abuser is in a mental state to change. A verbal agreement won't force the abuser to behave decently.

The relationship must be dynamic. While some partnerships are chosen, many relationships are forced upon people (like parents). Some relationships don't change; they merely get better with age. Others undergo significant alteration over time. Diverse emotions play a crucial role in relationships, which can serve as the best learning environment. Examine the relationship to see if it is emotionally healthy or traumatic.

5. Request expert assistance as necessary.

Relationships can still be maintained; leaving them is not the only choice. Investigate the additional angles that appear promising. A counselor's expert counsel might offer solace and reprieve. Using this, you can fight emotional crises that may manifest as personality changes, suicidal thoughts, and depression.

A support network offers a comprehensive method of treating misuse and its effects. In particular, when there is a risk to one's life, qualified therapy can relieve and professional guidance can prevent the toxic environment that fosters destructive thoughts.

In the worst case, if the abuser is excessively bothersome and demanding, breaking up may be your only option. Give your final effort careful consideration before attempting the impossible to avoid regrets in the future.

How to Respond to Verbal Harassment

Being the target of verbal abuse may be incredibly traumatic. Many victims believe they are to blame for their circumstances; thus, they typically remain passive and endure their suffering. To remain confident and guilt-free, verbal abuse must be dealt with as a serious offense.

1. Prevent retaliation

The situation may worsen if the victim responds to verbal abuse with even more passion and energy. At all costs, this must be avoided. In addition to making things risky, shouting and abusing one another will damage your reputation among coworkers and neighbors. It helps if one individual is calm and sensible. This does not, however, imply that you must constantly put up with verbal abuse.

Remaining silent if your partner verbally abuses you regularly will make things worse since it will give him/her an incentive. Most verbally abused victims are passive and do not respond for too long, which results in a great deal of pain and suffering. To see if the person can be subdued and stopped, verbal abuse must first be addressed in silence. Do not engage in argumentative discourse or counterattacks.

2. Maintain serenity.

If someone verbally abuses you, keep your cool and don't react violently. Of course, this would not be in the empath's nature. Determine what prompted the person to insult you verbally. It is useless to respond angrily and make things worse if your error caused him to react this way. You can explain your actions or offer an apology if you feel you have mistreated him after waiting until he or she has calmed down.

Your kind gesture will encourage him or her to quit abusing you verbally and enable them to become more composed. When things are under control, you may clarify and resolve the prevailing issues so they don't impact your interpersonal and professional connections.

Being abused makes it difficult to maintain composure and silence, though. It is beneficial to engage in relaxation techniques or take several deep breaths while counting to 10. Doing this can help you regain control and divert attention away from the verbal assault.

3. Ineffective baroque reaction

You may test this out with your family, close relatives, and coworkers. Bland baroque responses include superficial argumentation. Without specific points or justifications, it might be a foolish or dull debate only used to keep up with the individual. The individual verbally abusing you will typically grow bored or annoyed with you and leave you alone. A dull baroque reaction can only go on for 15 to 20 minutes before it loses effectiveness.

In these scenarios, you'll need to depart on your own accord. It's equally vital to avoid responding this way if your boss or another person you respect is verbally abusing you because it will just incite them to act violently. Additionally, it would give them the impression that you are trying to mock them and are being disrespectful.

Additionally, it would give them the impression that you are trying to mock them and are being disrespectful.

4. Avoid the Person at All Costs

If you've been practicing bland baroque responses to the abuser's insults for too long without results, or if the situation escalates, running away is your best bet before the abuser resorts to physical violence. One of the best ways to halt verbal abuse is to leave the room. If you are at fault and want to avoid a confrontation, it might not always work. If remaining composed and in control doesn't work, you can quickly leave the situation to end the verbal abuse. Remember that leaving the abusive situation can only temporarily stop it; you must be ready to confront the offender later and resolve the issue.

5. Request advice from friends

You may occasionally find yourself dealing with verbal abuse regularly in a marital or familial setting. In such circumstances, you may have already tried every available strategy to stop the verbal abuse without success. Ask your family members and friends for advice on the best course of action. You can contact organizations, domestic violence centers, or marriage counseling centers to discuss your situation and find out what has to be done to halt or stop such incidents from dragging you down.

How Do I Establish Boundaries?

There are many aspects of safety in life. Women need to feel safe and unafraid, including their physical, emotional, spiritual, and sexual well-being. Women are not safe if they believe they might be hurt or have already been hurt in any way, mainly at the hand of their spouse. Women should seek protection first, according to BTR, before "working on the (abusive) marriage." In short, women should feel safe and protected in their bodies, homes, and families.

Safety is a Right for All Women

We reaffirm that this is one of the most fundamental human rights and every woman deserves complete and entire safety since abuse jeopardizes security. Fortunately, boundaries can support women in seeking safety and starting the recovery process.

Boundaries Safeguard emotional abuse victims.

Marriage therapists have traditionally advised women to "establish boundaries" with their abusers by saying, "I will not be treated this way." The victim must follow through with a consequence that sends her abuser a message that she means business if the abuser continues to harm her. Tragically, because the action is made after the abuse has already occurred, it is ineffectual and even harmful because it does not stop the injury.

True boundaries shield victims from financial, sexual, emotional, and other relational abuse by preventing harmful conduct. When a boundary is successfully established, a victim recognizes a safety concern and then takes steps to safeguard herself against that concern being violated.

How do Boundaries Appear?

She can say, "I do not feel safe when my boyfriend yells at me," as an illustration. Simply state, "I'm moving in with my mother because I don't live with individuals who yell at me" could serve as the boundary. Or, "I will leave the room when I feel you are going to raise your voice."

Each woman will react differently to protect herself from damage; but in the end, she must take the necessary precautions to save herself. There is no single or best method to handle this situation, but every woman should remember that she has a right to feel safe. For clear advice on setting limits, consult a professional immediately.

Boundaries Protect Victims and Make Sure That Abusers Don't Change.

"Expecting someone to be truthful, accept responsibility, display humility, and submit to the repercussions of their conduct...These are fundamental abilities. It isn't complicated science, and you are not required to explain it to him." -Betrayal Trauma Recovery's founder, Anne Blythe.

When boundaries are viewed as the guardian of victims rather than a tool for changing abusers, they are most effective. It is the abuser's duty to change; the victim is not responsible for doing so. You have no power over what he does, and it is impossible to stop him from lying. Although you can make demands, you cannot [make him stop]. To avoid more abuse, you must remove yourself from the situation.

Set boundaries to protect your safety rather than to influence your partner.

It can be challenging for many women to utilize limits to ensure their safety and healing instead of using them to assist their partners. Because abusers tend to center their lives around themselves like narcissists, this is understandable and normal. Women can develop effective boundary-setting skills with the help of a solid support network, information about abuse and trauma, and qualified sympathetic assistance.

BTR Aids Victims in Setting and Upholding Boundaries

For victims of emotional abuse and pain caused by betrayal, getting help is crucial throughout the early phases of creating boundaries. As a Betrayal Trauma Recovery Group member, you will have a safe space to talk with others who are experiencing similar situations.

It's now simpler than ever to select a BTR Group session that works with your schedule without leaving your house, thanks to unrestricted access to more than fifteen meetings a week. A Certified Betrayal Trauma Specialist oversees each session.

What is The Purpose of a Boundary?

A boundary's primary function is to prevent harm. If you think of boundaries in the classic sense, you would have a fence or boundary line that prevents someone from crossing it. However, if the barrier does not prevent the injury, it is either a poor border or none. A border does not function improperly and doesn't help you much if you have a property line if someone can cross it without any issues.

I want you to see something that can truly stop the harm when I talk about boundaries. If you erect a fence, the boundary is still absent, but the abuser manages to scale it. You still don't have a border if you lock the fence, yet they still manage to scale it.

Boundaries That Prevent Damage

The reason why therapists and other "experts" have typically established boundaries in the following manner is why so many women are perplexed about them. When you say things like, "I won't tolerate pornography in my home" or "I won't be lied to," you're setting a boundary. It is your "border" there. After that, you must enforce your boundary if it is crossed.

Okay, that cycle of setting a boundary, having it violated, and then retaining or maintaining your barrier is troublesome. That is what a lot of therapists or coaches are currently advocating, but many women are finding it ineffective.

The BTR Boundaries Model

If that strategy works for you, keep it up and utilize it. However, if you've been instructed in using that approach and you're thinking, "This is difficult; how can I enforce my boundary?" When a boundary is "established," you say things like, "I will not be lied to," "I will not be treated this way," or "Porn is not allowed in my house," and when the barrier is crossed, you ask, "What do I do now?"

If this is the case, I suggest another approach to setting boundaries that is more practical and reasonable. Rather than being a statement of what you will and will not accept, think of a boundary as the real thing that stops harm from happening, whether physical or mental. If the injury is still occurring, tell yourself in your head that you don't yet have a boundary. You don't have a border if you believe that your property line serves as the limit, yet someone crosses it by walking over it.

Definition of a Boundary

The barrier is a fence, but the offender scales it. You don't currently have a boundary. The moment that person quits trespassing on your land, you can be sure that the boundary is indeed there.

You may wish to make some notes right now that a boundary truly stops the harm. A boundary's purpose is to prevent harm. You have not established a barrier if the damage continues. Understand that the goal is to stop the harm. What happens next if the harm doesn't stop? The circumstance is unchanged from before.

Statements are merely statements and cannot protect you.

BTR can assist you in identifying your safety needs and issues. You cannot stay secure uttering phrases like, "You cannot treat me this way" or "I will not accept this in my family." They are not a boundary. Making a list of things you will or will not tolerate while working on "boundary work" with a coach or therapist is not creating a list of boundaries. You are developing a list of safety-related concerns. These acts make me feel comfortable and do not make me feel safe.

You can put number one on your safety list, "I don't feel secure with someone who uses porn," for instance. Then comes, "I don't feel safe with someone who lies to me," as the second response. "I don't feel secure with someone who is grooming me through being kind to me when they actually just want to have sex" is the third response. "I don't feel safe when this or that" is the next statement.

Make a list of your safety concerns.

You might make a list similar to this, but that is a list of safety concerns rather than boundaries. Many women need to be aware of what safety entails. Most women haven't considered the questions: "What would help me feel safe? How do I feel more secure? What actions are secure, and which actions are risky?

Making a list of safety concerns is essential. You can put them in writing. Even your abuser can hear them from you. You may say, "I don't feel safe when you try to manipulate me," or "I don't feel safe when I'm gaslit." It truly doesn't matter if you say it or not. You should be informed of the potential dangers.

You can voice a safety concern and record it, but you cannot state a boundary since saying something like, "My border is this," has no effect. They can still almost scale the fence.

Setting boundaries is different from identifying safety issues.

I don't want anyone to believe that making a list of the things they will and won't tolerate will keep them safe. They will be able to recognize the harmful things with its assistance, which is undoubtedly a crucial first step, but it won't make you safer. Being able to identify an issue is to put a boundary around it. Your list of dangers is not a list of restrictions, but merely a summary.

Choose appropriate actions based on your safety concerns.

After you've learned about the potential dangers, you can make an informed decision about what you should do to protect yourself. These steps might be either mental or physical. Examples include writing something down, compiling a list of assertions, or identifying safety concerns. Note that you have not established limits if you have a list of things you will and will notpermit; you just made a list of potential safety problems.

Physical and mental actions: Limits are Actions.

It might only be a mental process, but set a boundary when you close your eyes. You might decide to go the other way. It may not necessarily indicate a divorce or a significant event. A boundary is an action that prevents harm. However, it can signify many other things.

Consider The Property Line as an Example.

When you set up a fence to stop someone from repeatedly crossing your property line, they climb over it. Due to the person's ability to cross the barrier, you still need one. Then you secure it with a lock, but this doesn't help as they can still scale the fence. You might decide to contact the police as your next move. "This individual is intruding on my land, so I'm calling the cops." The person is stopped by the police, who then imprison them and accuse them of trespassing. That may halt it, and once the hurt has decreased, you will know that you have a genuine barrier.

When I say that a boundary is an action, I mean exactly that. You can be positive you have a real barrier if the harm stops. For instance, banning someone on your phone prevents them from harassing you, calling, texting, and other similar actions. Can they now make a call from a different or blocked number? Yes, they can.

But if you set a rule that you won't pick up the phone when someone calls from a number you don't know, you'll never be caught off guard, and they'll have to leave a message. Are they going to leave an abusive message? They might, in which case you can keep blocking numbers and block that number.

Establish Boundaries That Meet Your Needs for Safety

Simply stating, "I won't talk to him," or "if he continues to lie and manipulate" doesn't keep you safe since he can lie and manipulate you during every conversation. Banning the abuser from your phone, blocking his emails, or deleting your social media accounts if you see he is breaching the boundary is a barrier because it stops the harm.

If it sounds too strict, you might set a lower boundary, such as leaving the room whenever he speaks or once he starts avoiding eye contact or refusing to engage in conversation. Does that prevent the damage? I'm still determining.

You must be aware of the harm. You can assess, "Okay, I set this boundary," which implies that you took action, and it ends if you have a list of the things that hurt you.

What is a Good Boundary for YOU?

Consider a scenario in which he is verbally abusing you in the car. You turn to stare out the window, at which point he pauses. If so, did it stop the harm? Is that a limit? There might be a yes to that question. Yes, it was successful because he immediately stopped. Okay, that's a nice border and now you can respond. You will observe that most abusers, particularly psychological abusers, tend to escalate their behavior once limits are established. You can tighten your limits when the abuse gets worse.

For a moment, let's discuss the distinction between borders and benchmarks. A boundary is a real action you take to stop the harm, either physically or mentally; whatever it is, you stop paying attention and become emotionally distant.

Benchmark – What is it?

You need to establish a standard to determine if the person is improving. They might begin revealing the truth at this point and have stopped lying to friends and family.

Note that a benchmark is not a boundary. Saying, "I'm going to set the boundary that he cannot move back home, and I'm going to change the locks. He needs to remain somewhere else," is an example of setting a boundary.

It's okay if this is your barrier, but you should set a clear criteria before he moves back in. If he enrolls in the Center for Peace (I'm just using it as an example), consider reevaluating your barrier.

"First stop the harm, then search for benchmarks."

Avoid putting the horse before the cart. Don't say to the offender, "Okay, if you don't go to Center for Peace, then you have to move out in three months" because if he doesn't, how will you get him out of the house when the three months have passed, and he hasn't signed up? It isn't easy. Even though getting him out of the house may be challenging, you must first set up the barrier.

Before locating the benchmark, stop the harm. Please don't wait to set a boundary and hope that benchmarks occur; don't look for them before the boundary has been established.

You are not required to express your boundaries orally. No. No. No. No. You'll only increase your risk to yourself. You can establish standards. You are under no obligation to inform the offender however. Say to yourself, "He knows about this and that, and he knows what to do, so I'm just not going to engage unless he engages in some of these behaviors."

It is not a complicated science. If he attends 12-Step, you don't have to tell him, "You can't move back in until this has happened" because he can figure it out if you're familiar with the 12-Steps and looking for a step 8 or 9 - like full restitution, making amends, or something else. He is a grown-up.

Only those benchmarks that you want to observe need to be stated. Expect the abuser to be truthful, accept responsibility, display humility, and submit to the results of their actions. These are fundamental abilities. It is not particularly complex, and you are not required to explain.

If you've already established the boundary before you look for the benchmarks, you'll be safe the entire time. If he wants to grow up and be an adult and healthy person, say "Great, I'll let him back into my life." If he doesn't, say, "Great, I'm safe,"

Boundaries Done Backwards

You must set your boundaries, which you must then communicate to the offender: "Okay, my boundary is no porn in the house. I will ask you to leave if you do porn in the house." That, in my opinion, is incorrect. You don't have to inform them or decide in advance if they use porn in your home. You can say, "You used porn in the house; you now need to move out" if it has become a safety problem.

Adults who are functioning, responsible, and mature don't require instructions such as, "If you lie to me, I feel unsafe, so I'm going to set a boundary." A mature and functioning adult would understand that lying to others is wrong.

Limits Have Two Components

1. a breach of safety.
2. a mechanism—physical or mental—that prevents harm.
The rule: Safety violation>Boundary to stop the harm.

Whether or not he comprehends it, you can still take action and build a barrier to protect yourself. You are not required to explain its purpose. Simply define the boundaries to ensure your safety. If he receives it, fine but if not, he does not. You are not required to make an effort to explain it to him.

It's not difficult to teach someone to behave honestly, avoid manipulation, avoid pornography, and refrain from cheating. Adults should be able to perform these fundamental tasks, and you are not required to explain.

Pay Attention to Manipulation

It is pure manipulation to persuade you to communicate with someone who isn't safe, or if someone tries to make you feel it is your job. COVID-19 is intriguing because of all the apocalyptic "end of the world" discussions going on. I'm not claiming that this is the end of the world as I have no idea, yet verses 10 and 11 of the Bible say the following:

Because the time is rapidly approaching when the Lord God will cause a great divide among the people and slay the wicked; nevertheless, he will spare his people, even if it means using fire.

And the girdle of his loins shall be righteousness, and the girdle of his reins, faithfulness.

Limits are Godly and Healthy

Throughout the Bible, this separation between the wicked or ill and the healthy is foretold. I just recorded a podcast on limits and passages from the New Testament that discuss boundaries. It's not true if you're a lady of faith and say, "Well, hold on a second, this lack of communication or distancing feels horrible, and my church doesn't teach this."

The scriptures support this in several places. That there will be a sharp separation between the wicked and the righteous in the final days and is an acceptable belief if you notice wickedness or disease in your own home and say, "Wait a minute, I need to separate myself from this."

Protecting Yourself From Danger

If you have COVID-19, it's equivalent to going into quarantine. Even with today's public health concerns, it is a safety issue for everyone. I'm not suggesting having it makes you evil. If you have the virus, you should keep your distance from those who don't know so you don't spread. The same is true of wickedness.

Don't believe that I think those who have COVID-19 are sinners or bad. Please don't take that from this example, but in the case of injury, it's critical to keep yourself separate from harm; otherwise, you risk becoming harmed. Apart from removing yourself from it, there is no other method of self-defense.

Setting Boundaries vs. Identifying Safety Issues

What is a boundary? I want the answer to be, "A boundary is a protective barrier." Let's assume you tell the asker when you're fighting with them, "If you don't speak to me with respect, I am not going to participate in the dialogue." Although you haven't established a boundary, you have pointed out a safety concern and said what you would do. That doesn't define a boundary.

If you are participating in the conversation and someone is not treating you with respect, the boundary would leave the room. If you continue to interact with someone injuring you, even after repeatedly asking them to stop or pleading with them, you have not halted the harm.

A Boundary is a Wall That Reduces the Effects of the Damage

How do boundaries work? The reply is, "It is a wall that prevents harm. You should compile a list of safety issues or worries to decide what obstacles you require or what harms exist in your life. These are the actions I am observing that raise safety concerns; I don't want them in my house. The concern is safety.

Boundaries are not Requests

It's not a barrier if it is merely a safety issue if a woman wants her husband to seek therapy. So she "establishes a boundary" and tells him, "You can only have a male therapist." She is worried does not want him to see a female therapist because she does not want him to be alone with another woman. She makes it clear: "I don't want you to have a female therapist." She has every right to prevent her husband from spending time alone with other women, including a therapist since he has shown a pattern of cheating and deceit. What would you do to ensure your safety in that situation?

She needs to remove herself from the situation to end the harm, perhaps by saying, "Well, he chooses to go to a female therapist, but my boundary is going to be definite. I'm going to stay with my mom because every time I see him, I'm triggered to feel unsafe."

Take another example: a woman just learned that her spouse has been watching porn virtually every day for the previous month. "It is so disappointing," she remarks. Of course, his only response is to apologize. In response, she says, "I am aware of his regret, but how does it alter anything?"

A question would follow from an empath or therapist: "I'm very sorry that you feel sad that your husband has been using porn. What limit might help you feel emotionally safe in your own home?" This is a boundary response. If he left, would you feel more secure? Would sleeping in a different room make you feel safer? What will you do to protect yourself from his vicious behavior?"

There are two steps to using the BTR model for boundaries:

Part 1: A violation of safety or an abusive act would involve lying, gaslighting, manipulating, using porn, engaging in extramarital sex, engaging in affairs, or engaging in any other abusive activity.

Part 2: A border, sometimes known as a safety barrier, is your action to prevent someone from hurting you, like turning away, closing your eyes, walking away, segregating yourselves, or sleeping in separate bedrooms.

Is a Boundary a Protective Barrier?

Does it harm society if someone in Brazil solicits a prostitute and you don't know them or the prostitute? Yes, but is it causing you harm? No. I suppose it indirectly hurts us all. However, it upsets you greatly if your husband is courting a prostitute.

You're trying to push his conduct as far away from you as possible because that would stop the pain. You try to get enough room in your thoughts and heart to say, "What he does is far away from me." If something is close to you, it will always cause you damage, so try to distance yourself as much as possible.

You are powerless over what the abuser does.

What if there is nothing you can do despite your best efforts. How do you get away so his actions don't hurt you anymore? The new approach is to eliminate the necessity for "enforcing" the barrier to make it feel less restrictive. If someone crosses your boundary, you have to "enforce" it, which leaves you feeling, "Oh no, I told him, and he crossed that limit, now what do I do? This is the fundamental issue that everyone is experiencing.

Boundaries Reduce His Negative Behavior's Impact

Because you don't have to worry about enforcing anything in the new approach, it doesn't quite function as well as the two-part model of a safety violation and a boundary. You act to protect yourself from the lies after experiencing a safety violation caused by them. You cease speaking to him since, if he tells you a lie, the only way to halt the harm is to stop talking to him.

"Separating yourself is the only thing you can do."

There is no alternative strategy. It is impossible to stop him from lying. Keep your distance from known liars is all you can do.

Why do Boundaries Exist and How Can I Protect Myself?"

If the traditional approach works but you still need to figure out a boundary, keep asking. How can I protect myself? "This new boundary model of safety breach will help you. To sum up, a boundary is a safeguard that prevents harm. He could still engage in harmful activities, but he can no longer hurt you since the established barrier protects you.

The actual harm is significantly diminished.

Does he intend to harm you? Yes, now you can erect the protection barrier, but he can still carry out his evil deeds. Will you still feel pain? Yes. Even if he is lying to others about you and other things, the harm to you is significantly lessened when you are not in contact.

Bringing up and discussing safety-related issues and concerns is helpful, but if you don't do anything to protect your safety, merely talking about it or compiling a list won't do much good.

Key Findings

- Abuse of any kind, whether mental, sexual, or physical, can have serious psychological consequences. It's crucial to evaluate a physical abuser's mental health and seek any undiagnosed mental disorders. Leaving an abusive relationship is difficult, especially if there are children present, and a mean or narcissistic person may be able to change their conduct and mental state through counseling. Before you take the drastic measure of ending your relationship with a physically abusive person, you should explore counseling.
- Numerous psychiatric issues are simple to treat with counseling. Deeply ingrained issues can be discovered. There is no opportunity for happiness or growth in an abusive relationship. It is in everyone's best interest to take precautions against emotional trauma as soon as possible.
- There are a few strategies for handling emotional abuse that can help protect you and your partner from harm. Abuse might result from insecurity or a lack of trust, and the situation could worsen if you miss or cannot detect abusive behavior. An easy target is a vulnerable or empathic victim, such as a youngster subjected to emotional abuse by a parent.
- Both sides should accept the principles for reestablishing mutual respect. Being the target of verbal abuse may be incredibly traumatic. To remain confident and guilt-free, verbal abuse must be dealt with as a serious offense. A support network offers a comprehensive method for treating misuse and its effects. Professional guidance can prevent the toxic environment that fosters destructive thoughts.
- If someone verbally abuses you, keep your cool and don't react violently. Most verbally abused victims are passive

and do not respond for long, which results in a great deal of pain and suffering.
- It is beneficial to engage in some relaxation techniques or take several deep breaths while counting to 10. You may test this out with your family, close relatives, and coworkers. A dull baroque reaction can only go on for 15 to 20 minutes before it loses effectiveness.
- It's equally vital to avoid responding if your boss or another person you respect is verbally abusing you. Women need to feel safe and unafraid in all aspects of their lives, including their physical, emotional, spiritual, and sexual well-being. Women are not secure if they believe they might be hurt or have already been hurt in any way. It is often when their spouse indulges in offensive pornography.

9

WHAT IS CODEPENDENCY?

Each partner in a relationship may be dependent on the other on a mental, emotional, physical, and/or spiritual level. This is described as being a codependent. Couples who are codependent can also depend on their friends and family.

This dependency is frequent in marriages where one partner suffers from an addiction to alcohol or drugs. The concept originated in the study of chemical dependence. "The phrase was originally coined in the 1950s, within the framework of Alcoholics Anonymous, to support partners of those who misused substances and who were intertwined in the toxic lives of those they cared about," explains Dr. Renee Exelbert, a certified psychologist and author based in New York.

Codependency: the APA Definition

Codependence is defined by the American Psychological Association (APA) as "abusive dependency, a pattern of interactions in which one person is psychologically reliant on (or dominated by) another with a mental illness (examples: alcoholism, gambling)."

Codependency is not a formalized personality disorder or a professional diagnosis in and of itself. In general, it contains elements of early childhood attachment-type patterns. Other personality disorders such as dependent personality disorder and codependency can coexist.

Causes of Codependency

What causes codependency in the first place? Inadequate boundaries and a poor sense of one's worth contribute significantly, as does a lack of confidence in one's own opinions and the inability to assert one's will.

According to research, codependency may be influenced by biological, psychological, and social factors:

- Biological: a codependent person's prefrontal cortex region of the brain may not be able to control their empathetic reactions. As a result, there would be an excess of empathy, facilitating codependency.
- Psychological: codependents may have a psychological propensity to care for others. Adverse life events, such as having divorced parents or being neglected or subjected to emotional abuse, can also impact mental health.
- Social: changes in society's perception of women's roles or a rise in drug abuse prevalence in families can contribute to codependency.

Codependency can take on a variety of forms and levels of severity. Dr. Mayfield adds that it can manifest itself in other kinds of partnerships. It can occur in relationships between parents and children, partners, spouses, coworkers, and superiors. It may be particularly apparent in certain empaths.

Signs of Codependency

An unbalanced pattern of relationships is referred to as codependency. One person takes on the burden of taking care of the needs of another without taking any time to acknowledge their own needs or feelings.

Codependency manifests itself when one person has an intense desire to be needed by another and vice versa. The enabler, also known as "the taker," makes sacrifices for the codependent person, also known as "the giver," who feels worthless without their need.

Therefore, codependent relationships are built on an imbalance of power that serves the taker's demands. The provider is then free to continue giving, frequently at their own expense.

According to Drs. Mayfield and Exelbert, codependency can show a variety of symptoms. Some may indicate that you are the caretaker in a codependent relationship:

- Feeling as though you're "stepping on eggshells" around the other person to prevent confrontation.
- Needing to check in with the other person or get their permission to carry out daily duties.
- Frequently being the one to apologize, even when you did nothing wrong.
- Having sympathy for the other person despite their wrongdoing.
- Consistently attempting to change or save problematic, addicted, or poorly functioning individuals whose issues are too complex for one person to handle.
- Making an effort to help others, even if it makes you uncomfortable.
- Placing someone else in a superior position while they are undeserving of it.
- A yearning to be liked by others to feel good about yourself.

- Finding it challenging to find any alone time, especially if all your free time is spent with someone else.
- Sensing like you've lost your sense of self because of the relationship.

Reasons Codependency is Dangerous

Everyone has loved ones and therefore feels some level of responsibility for them; but putting too much value on the views of others can cause emotional and mental distress. Codependency refers only to those caring behaviors or feelings that are excessive to an undesirable degree. Both self-responsibility and responsibility for interactions with others must coexist.

The pattern of relating has been called a "relationship addiction" because codependents so often choose partners who are emotionally and/or physically violent. Since the giver invests so much in the taker, codependency has the inherent problem of making the giver forget their actual sense of self. Even if the donor doesn't feel this way right away—they probably enjoy providing their affection and being relied upon—as the relationship develops, it can reach harmful levels.

Another problem with codependency is that it becomes challenging for the provider to quit the relationship because they may believe the recipient depends on them so heavily, even though they intuitively know it is the proper thing to do. In contrast, the taker will feel so dependent on the provider that they may find it challenging to end a toxic relationship.

Getting Rid of Codependency

Focusing on self-awareness is the first step in overcoming codependent behavior. Of course, you can accomplish this on your own. However, Dr. Mayfield also emphasizes the value of counseling to help you overcome your codependent tendencies. "Many codependents wait until their lives are in danger before seeking therapy," "Dr. Mayfield explains. "I would say to be proactive and ask for assistance.

When you start that adventure, do your best to follow these guidelines:

- Learn to speak to yourself with love and positivity and fight the need to critique yourself.
- Start with baby steps toward relationship separation. Take part in extracurricular activities and make an effort to make new friends. Determine the characteristics that define you, then elaborate on them.
- When you are inclined to contemplate or worry about someone else, consciously focus on yourself. Be patient with yourself as you get better at this.
- Dr. Exelbert advises, "Stand up for yourself if someone criticizes, undercuts, or tries to control you." You'll become stronger in yourself if you work on boosting your self-esteem.
- If you don't want to do anything, don't be afraid to say "no."
- If one-on-one counseling doesn't appeal to you, try a support group or group psychotherapy.

There is also a group called Codependents Anonymous (CoDa) that deals with the dynamics of previous relationships and the need to be needed.

There are many variations and degrees of codependency. It frequently results in a toxic interpersonal dynamic that deteriorates over time as the codependent person (the giver) loses their identity.

The first stage is to identify codependency warning indicators. Then lessening your codependent tendencies and engaging in self-awareness and active redirection are crucial. The process of altering years of habit should be approached with compassion.

Key Findings

- Each partner in a relationship who is dependent on the other on a mental, emotional, physical, and spiritual level is said to be codependent.
- Some symptoms may indicate that you are the caretaker in a codependent relationship: feeling as though you're "stepping on eggshells" around the other person to prevent confrontation and needing to check in with the other person or get their permission to carry out daily duties. In addition, frequently being the one to apologize, even when you did nothing wrong.
- Getting rid of codependency entails focusing on self-awareness is the first step.
- Learn to speak to yourself with love and positivity.
- Be patient with yourself as you get better at this.
- You'll grow stronger if you work on boosting your self-esteem.
- To lessen codependent tendencies, after self-awareness, active redirection is crucial.

10

IMPROVING EMOTIONAL INTELLIGENCE (EQ)

When it comes to achieving success and fulfillment in life, EQ is on par with intelligence. Find out how to improve your emotional quotient, fortify your bonds with others, and accomplish your objectives.

What exactly is EQ or emotional intelligence?

Emotional intelligence is the ability to identify, label, and manage one's emotions effectively for the purpose of stress management, effective communication, empathic understanding, problem-solving, and conflict resolution (EQ). You can develop well-built relationships, perform well at work and school, and reach your professional and personal objectives with the help of your emotional intelligence. Additionally, it can assist you in establishing a connection with your emotions, putting your intentions into practice, and choosing what is most important to you. It is a particularly valuable process for an empath. But the narcissist will sneer and walk away.

Four characteristics frequently used to characterize emotional intelligence:

1. Self-management - You restrain irrational thoughts and actions, regulate your emotions healthily, take the initiative, keep your word, and adjust to changing situations.
2. Self-awareness – You know your feelings and how they influence your actions and thinking. You are confident in yourself and are aware of your talents and flaws.
3. Social awareness – You have empathy. You can discern emotional indicators, comprehend the needs and worries of others, feel at ease in social situations, and comprehend the power relationships in a team or organization.
4. Relationship management - You understand how to create and build strong bonds with people, express yourself clearly, motivate and influence others, collaborate well, and handle disagreements.

What makes emotional IQ so crucial?

We all know that the most successful and contented individuals are only sometimes the most intelligent. You might know someone who excels academically but is socially awkward and unproductive at work or in personal relationships. Your intelligence quotient (IQ) or intellectual prowess is insufficient to lead a successful life. If you want to attend an elite school, a high IQ will work in your favor. Still, it is emotional intelligence (EQ) that will help you stay calm and collected under pressure during your final exams. IQ and EQ go hand in hand and work best when complementing one another.

You can lead and inspire people, succeed in your job, and negotiate the social complexity of the workplace with high emotional intelligence. Many businesses now prioritize emotional intelligence above technical competence when evaluating key job prospects and conducting EQ tests before hiring.

What EQ entails:

<u>Your bodily well-being</u>. If you can't control your emotions, likely, you can't handle stress. Serious health issues may result. Unmanaged stress increases blood pressure, weakens the immune system, boosts the risk of heart attacks and strokes, affects fertility, and hastens the onset of age. Managing stress is the first step in increasing emotional intelligence.

<u>Your emotional well-being</u>: stress and unchecked emotions can negatively affect your mental health and put you at risk for depression and anxiety. Strong connections will be difficult to establish if you cannot comprehend, accept, or manage your emotions. This will further aggravate existing mental health issues and leave you feeling alone and alone.

<u>Your connections</u>. You can better articulate how you and others feel if you are better aware of your emotions and how to control them. As a result, you can build deeper relationships and communicate more effectively in your personal and professional life.

<u>Your social awareness</u>. Understanding your emotions helps you connect with others and the outside world socially. You can discern a friend from an enemy, gauge another person's interest in you, relieve stress, regulate your nervous system through social interaction, and feel loved and happy thanks to social intelligence.

Four essential abilities to develop emotional intelligence (EQ)

Emotional intelligence is a set of abilities that can be learned at any moment. It's important to remember that simply understanding EQ differs from putting it into practice. Even though you may be aware that you ought to do something, stress can sometimes overpower your best efforts, making it difficult to follow through. You must learn how to handle stress in the present and your relationships to maintain emotional awareness if you want to alter your behavior in ways that hold up permanently under pressure.

The following are the main competencies for raising EQ, enhancing emotional regulation, and increasing social interaction:

1. Self-management
2. Self-awareness
3. Social conscience
4. Relationship administration

1. Self-management is the first crucial skill for developing emotional intelligence.

To put your EQ to good use, you must master allowing your emotions to guide your decisions. Overstressing might make it difficult for you to maintain control over your emotions and make wise decisions. Consider a period when tension ultimately overcame you. Was it simple to make a decision or think clearly? Most likely not. Overstress impairs your capacity for clear thinking and correct emotional assessment, both your own and other people's.

Emotions are obvious indicators of who you are, but when faced with the kind of stress that pushes us beyond our comfort zones, we may get overwhelmed and lose control of our emotions. You can learn to take in painful information without allowing it to take control of your thoughts and self-control if you can moderate the tension and remain emotionally present. You'll be able to make decisions while regulating impulsive thoughts and actions, deal with your emotions in healthier ways, take charge, keep your word, and adjust to changing situations.

2. Self-awareness

Building emotional intelligence requires more than just managing stress. According to the science of attachment, your current emotional state reflects what you went through in infancy. Your capacity for controlling fundamental emotions like sadness, joy, fear, and rage is frequently influenced by the caliber and constancy of your early emotional experiences. Your emotions would be valuable assets in adult life if your primary caregiver as an infant recognized and cherished them. However, if you had perplexing, frightening, or painful emotional experiences as a baby, you may have made an effort to suppress your feelings.

The secret to knowing how emotion affects your ideas and actions is connecting to your emotions—having a moment-to-moment connection with your shifting emotional experience.

Do you ever feel as though your emotions are in a continual state of flux, changing as your experiences do? Do you have any bodily feelings in your chest, throat, or stomach that go along with your emotions? Do you have distinct sensations and emotions like anger, sadness, fear, or joy, all expressed subtly through facial expressions?

Can you have feelings that are so strong they hold both your and other people's attention? Do you give your feelings any thought? Do they influence how you decide?

If any of these situations are unusual, you may have "turned down" or "shut off" your emotions. You must acknowledge, embrace, and get comfortable with your fundamental emotions to improve your emotional intelligence (EQ) and become emotionally healthy. This is something that mindfulness practice can help you with.

Focusing on the present moment on purpose and without passing judgment constitutes the practice of mindfulness. Buddhism originated from mindfulness, but most world religions practice similar forms of prayer or meditation. With mindfulness, you may change your focus from being preoccupied with thoughts to appreciating the present and your physical and emotional experiences and gaining a broader perspective on life. As you become more focused and at peace, you become more self-aware.

Its critical first to learn stress management techniques to feel more at ease, reconnect with strong or uncomfortable emotions, and alter how you perceive and react to your feelings. You can use the free

Emotional Intelligence Toolkit from HelpGuide to increase your emotional awareness.

3. Social awareness

You can identify and decipher the primarily nonverbal clues that people use to communicate with you by engaging in social awareness. The indicators enable you to understand how others genuinely feel, how their emotional state shifts over time, and what matters most to them. You can read and comprehend a group's power dynamics and shared emotional experiences when they exhibit similar nonverbal clues.

Emotional and social intelligence are allies of mindfulness.

You must comprehend the significance of mindfulness in the social process if you want to develop social awareness. After all, you can't pick up on tiny nonverbal signs when you're lost in your thoughts, distracted by other thoughts, or just zoning out on your phone. Present-day awareness is necessary for social awareness. While many of us take pleasure in our ability to multitask, doing so means you'll miss the subtle emotional changes that other people are going through and how these changes might help you completely comprehend them.

Actually, putting other thoughts aside and concentrating on the contact itself increases your chances of achieving your social objectives. To follow the flow of another person's emotional reactions, you must also be aware of the changes in your own emotional experience. Being aware of others doesn't make you less self-aware. In attentively listening to others, you may learn new and intriguing things about yourself, your values, and your worldview. For instance, you will have discovered something significant about yourself if you find it uncomfortable to hear others voice their particular viewpoints.

4. Relationship management

Working productively with others requires emotional awareness and the capacity to identify and comprehend what other people are going through. Once emotional awareness is present, you can effectively learn new social and emotional skills to improve your interactions' quality, quantity, and effectiveness.

Learn to be conscious of your nonverbal communication skills. It is impossible to avoid conveying your thoughts and feelings to other people through nonverbal cues. The numerous muscles in your face, particularly those surrounding your eyes, nose, lips, and forehead, should allow you to read the emotions of others and express your feelings without using words. Even if you disregard the signals from your emotional brain, others won't. Relationship improvement can be greatly aided by being aware of the nonverbal cues you convey to others.

Play and have fun while destressing. Play, laughing, and humor are all effective stress relievers; they lighten your load and assist you in maintaining perspective. Laughter balances your neurological system, lowering tension, calming you down, focusing your thinking, and increasing your capacity for empathy.

Recognize that disagreements can bring people closer together. In human interactions, conflict and disagreement are unavoidable. Two people cannot always share the same wants, beliefs, and expectations. That needn't be a terrible thing. Building trust among people can result from conflict resolution that is productive and healthy. Conflict encourages freedom, creativity, and safety in relationships when not seen as threatening or punishing.

Key Findings

- Find out how to improve your emotional quotient, fortify your bonds with others, and accomplish your objectives.
- You must acknowledge, embrace, and get comfortable with your fundamental emotions to improve your

emotional intelligence (EQ) and become emotionally healthy.
- Emotional and social intelligence are allies of mindfulness.
- You must comprehend the significance of mindfulness in the social process if you want to develop social awareness.
- Your present-day awareness is necessary for social awareness.
- Being aware of others doesn't make you less aware of yourself.
- Learn to be conscious of your nonverbal communication skills.

11

SIX SELF-CARE STRATEGIES FOR DEALING WITH TRAUMA

Although traumatic experiences are incredibly upsetting, they need not define your identity forever. It might be challenging to overcome the trauma caused by abuse, but it is possible. Here are six things you may do to aid with your recovery.

1. Be Aware of the Trauma's Effects

Abuse contributes to many of trauma's impacts. Common side effects include:

- Sleep issues
- Anxiety and panic attacks
- Use of drugs
- Eating problems
- Recollections of physical or sexual abuse
- Self-hatred and low self-esteem feelings
- Fear of relationships and people
- Suicidal ideas

Address the trauma and seek professional assistance if you experience any warning signals.

2. Understand the Importance of Healing

Healing is essential for overcoming trauma. While the specific steps to overcome past hurts and undergo healing may vary, the desire to do so is common. Some guidelines:

- Let the victims concentrate on themselves. Sometimes, negative emotions and thoughts might become overwhelming. However, with healing, survivors can divert their attention from the bad and pay attention to what they need in the moment.
- Enable survivors to establish closer bonds with others. Let your loved ones be your support network while participating in the healing process.
- Assist survivors in discovering ways to cope with their sorrow, such as taking a new pastime, picking up old interests, spending more time outside, etc.
- Ais survivors in feeling new emotions after releasing all the emotions from traumatic situations.

3. Use positive affirmations.

Beginning with "forcing" the positive will help to refocus the subconscious mind. Your inner critic or negativity can encourage self-sabotage and prevent you from accepting good things. You can refocus this inner critic by implementing empowering affirmations that you may employ daily. Positive affirmations can stop those unwanted and disruptive thoughts and change them into something constructive. Try the following optimistic affirmations:

- "I cherish myself."

SIX SELF-CARE STRATEGIES FOR DEALING WITH TRAUMA

- "I am deserving."
- "I am lovely."

4. Workout

Additionally, physical healing of the mind is possible. Find at least one easy-to-do activity that forces you let go of the sadness, wrath, and hurt resulting from the fallout from abuse and trauma. Here are some excellent workouts to try:

- Running
- Yoga
- Dance cardio
- Kickboxing

The best aspect abut this is that you can play uplifting music or affirmations while you work out. Just keep in mind that exercise should help, not hurt you.

5. Embrace Creativity

Art therapy has demonstrated benefits for PTSD patients by allowing patients to create and integrate. In a 2018 study, the National Center for Biotechnology Information (NCBI) instructed a group of volunteers to produce artwork based on a specific theme throughout eight sessions lasting 75 minutes (i.e., nature, religion, colors). According to NCBI, most study participants "showed regression in their drawings of the trauma or the aftermath" after receiving this art therapy. Therefore, by producing something, you can express yourself in a transforming way and let go of the trauma and its adverse effects.

The following are some fantastic exercises you can perform as part of art therapy:

- Arts & crafts
- writing
- drawing
- painting
- performing or creating music

By producing something, you can either share it with the world or keep it as a constant inspiration.

6. Don't be afraid to ask for assistance.

Finally, make a help request. You are not rendered weak or impotent by this, and your willingness to ask for and accept assistance demonstrates bravery. Find a mental health practitioner who will validate your experience. Choose someone knowledgeable about trauma. Additionally, you can locate a group of survivors that share your perspective. You can get more assistance through the National Domestic Violence Hotline.

Even though the path to rehabilitation is rarely simple or quick, the work is always worthwhile. Learning and healing have no time restrictions; all it takes is one tiny step at a time.

Key Findings

- Be aware that trauma's effects may entail abuse.
- Understand the importance of healing. It's crucial to understand that healing is essential for overcoming trauma.
- Use positive affirmations.
- Embracing creativity art therapy has demonstrated benefits for PTSD patients by allowing patients to create and integrate.
- The following are some fantastic exercises you can perform as part of art therapy: Arts & crafts, writing,

drawing, painting, performing, or creating music. By producing something, you can either share it with the world or keep it as a constant inspiration.
- Don't be afraid to ask for assistance.
- Finally, make a help request.

12

A MANUAL FOR MINDFUL SELF-CARE PRACTICE

As crucial as looking after those we care about most ensures that our needs are satisfied, we must consider ourselves. It can be difficult to focus on oneself, but there are easy ways to overcome the discomfort. Self-care entails being honest about what you need and acting on that response. It can be as easy as going to bed early after a long day at work or as challenging as examining some of your behaviors and their long-term implications with a friend of therapist.

Self-Care: What Is It?

Self-care is the practice of actively promoting personal happiness, looking out for our own well-being, and being able to respond to stressful situations without becoming unbalanced or experiencing a health emergency. Self-care entails being honest about what you need and meeting those needs.

The Development of Self-Care

The "radical" idea of self-care emerged during the civil rights movement when valiant people battled the tenacious foes of prejudice and discrimination. Together, these American heroes overcame insurmountable obstacles and horrible treatment to establish the first authentic communities of caring.

We shouldn't forget that one of the ideas they fought for was and still is the fundamental human right to care for oneself. Treatment for people of color was frequently refused in hospitals and healthcare facilities, and the federal government abandoned the policy. Self-care essentially becomes a life-or-death situation. The only support they could find was in each other and inside themselves as they fought a hard war.

In sum, the civil rights movement gave birth to the fundamental concept of being able to take care of oneself and having the time, money, and resources required to do so.

How to Create a Movement for Self-Care

1) Let's immediately remove the stigma from mental health. We need to adopt a new perspective on mental health and guarantee that everyone has access to the support systems, means of transportation, services, and resources required to deal with mental health appropriately.

2) Make a promise to impart your understanding of self-care. Everybody faces daily responsibilities and unique difficulties. However, let's give up trying to do it alone. We're creating communities of caring and igniting the self-care revolution when we make time in our schedules for others, plan and attend social events with friends, and even send a few meaningful emails.

. . .

3) Assist in setting the criteria. Lack of definition is a major factor in our culture's sluggish embrace of self-care. Because self-care standards have never been formally created, we are unsure as to what they should be. By giving them a clear path to follow, defining self-care standards will legitimize our cause. Based on attainable and realistic goals, they'll be able to build a strategy, track their progress, and adjust it as needed.

4) Recognize that ineffective leadership results from exhaustion. Not precisely the trait of a great leader, fatigue reduces the attention span and increases emotional instability and poor decision-making. Because of this, our efforts to pioneer the self-care movement must be long-lasting. If we burn out, our employees, volunteers, kids, and other people in our circle of influence will do the same. We must be willing to set an example of a manageable pace of work if we are to foster a culture of self-care.

5) We need to ask ourselves important questions to change our self-care behaviors and those of people around us, which will help us move from reflection to action and generate momentum for climbing the next peak. These queries could be:

- How does my lack of self-care affect the effectiveness of my leadership?
- Which habit(s) negatively affect my ability to take care of myself, and what new behavior can I replace them with?
- Have I shared my self-care plan with people who can hold me accountable and put one in place to ensure I follow through on this new behavior?
- How will I keep tabs on my development along the way?
- How can I help my employees, volunteers, friends, and family succeed?

Instead of being a reaction to burnout, the current self-care movement needs to begin as a prevention practice. The movement must demand that people prioritize their health and well-being without feeling guilty.

Why is Self-Care Important?

When you find yourself perched on the edge of a cliff, staring into the black abyss, self-care can be a lifesaving intervention that prevents you from entirely getting dragged into the vortex.

You Need a Self-Care Plan for 3 Reasons

Created by you, a self-care plan is a failsafe that includes your preferred self-care practices, significant reminders, and strategies for energizing your self-care community. Here are some reasons why you should make your self-care plan:

1) Creating a personalized self-care plan is a protective measure. While you're not in a crisis, you can direct your best self to consider what you might require (and have access to) during the most difficult times. Only you know your limits regarding stress and what resources you have available to you.

2) In an emergency, knowing what to do and who to contact is far less stressful when the preparation has been made ahead of time. From a mindfulness perspective, it enables you to respond to the current event instead of simply reacting to it. When you have a plan in place, your life will feel less chaotic, and you will feel more in control of your circumstances. (It also simplifies asking folks who know about your assistance plan.)

. . .

3) A self-care plan aids in maintaining perseverance. You'll find it much simpler to follow your care plan and avoid the excuse-making snare. Making a plan aid in creating a routine and preventing isolation for you and your self-care partners. Instead, you can communicate often, hold one another accountable, and take turns being there for one another.

Making a Self-Care Plan: a Guide

Keep a map of your self-care strategy in your back pocket. It's there to help you walk the talk and assist you in returning to equilibrium by offering a clear path back home if you get off course.

1) Start by compiling a list of activities based on the various aspects of your life. One of the simplest methods to get started is to divide this overwhelming work into multiple categories, such as:

- Work
- Physical Fitness
- Community and Relationships
- Emotional Life

Write down the methods or techniques you can use that are true to who you are and advance your well-being in each of the areas above.

A few options include:

- Hanging out with friends.
- Being physically active.
- Practicing mindfulness.
- Developing the self-assurance to set appropriate boundaries (here's a form).

Be creative, have fun, and most importantly, be honest about what works and doesn't work for you.

2) Next, write down potential challenges and the strategies for overcoming them. Ask yourself what obstacles might prevent you from completing each action as you list them.

3) Tell your closest pals about your strategy. Remember to rely on your community of care and your network of self-care friends.

Using Self-Care Techniques

Neither "fighting" nor "fleeing" is sustainable, which is the central point of the argument. Furthermore, they are reactions we may outgrow. We frequently hear that "we evolved this way" and our brains are hardwired for fight-or-flight responses, yet we know that evolution is ongoing. Our minds are rewireable.

How can we move past the fight-or-flight response? By shifting toward two new reactions: action and empathy. They all begin with self-care.

Several Techniques for Self-Care Today

To refuel, renew, and rewire for action, grassroots meditation activist, Shelly Tygielski, provides three strategies to practice self-care.

1. Permit yourself to (finally) disconnect from social media and the news for a few days. Don't use social media; switch off your alerts, push notifications, and turn off the TV. Limit your time if you have to access it for business or another reason, and avoid leaving comments. It only lasts a few days. It is so peaceful when unplugged.

. . .

2. Acknowledge when you require self-care, and then attend to it. Care for the self occasionally benefits individuals in the immediate vicinity (You may need to arrange a babysitter or request time off from work.). Let everyone around you know that you are attending to a personal need without seeking their approval.

3. Prepare a self-care checklist with a ton of alternatives that are personalized especially for you. These self-care techniques might include everything from taking a bubble bath to setting up a mid-day phone call with a buddy. It is crucial to have this list prepared because you might need help in thinking of the care possibilities when you are close to burning out.

Learning to Say, "I Need Help," is the Most Courageous Self-Care Act.

Do you tend to forget to fill your gas tank when the low fuel light comes on because you're too busy getting from one location to another? Too hurried to stop for a moment? Are you too ashamed to take a break, even if it's obvious you need one? Maybe you feel you need to feel stronger to ask for a break. Or you're too preoccupied with getting through your day to notice all the cues indicating it's time to take a break, breathe, and evaluate the issue.

It's important to recognize when a "personal moment" is required. Most of us are already rather adept at this part of the equation. When acting on our own recognition, we frequently need to catch up. Just being aware of the low gasoline indicator inside your thoughts is insufficient. You must obey its instructions to stop, park, and refill by pulling over. This can be complicated and frequently calls for much personal bravery.

Three Self-Care Techniques to Take Back Your Healing Time

Name-it-to-Tame-It: The Confession Statement

The "name-it-to-tame it" or "confession statement" method is about sharing your anxieties with a trusted friend or loved one and then allowing yourself to accept and embrace them. An example of a confessional statement: "I'm afraid to admit this, but I need to take a step back. To obtain mental and spiritual clarity, I require some solitude."

You, the confessor, discover a friendly and understanding ear. Your confidant is relieved of the burdens that prevent you from taking care of yourself since they know they are being trusted with your vulnerability. All in all, things are feeling quite fantastic.

The Pre-Ask: requesting assistance or room before you require it

Most people wait until their anxiety is at its worst before they ask for assistance or admit they need space. Let's return to the example of the "low fuel" indicator. You can only go around 30 miles before running out of gas after the light turns on. Still, that's 30 miles away. There's no immediate need to start looking for a petrol station. Why stress over what might occur in the future, you might ask. This light is activated by the accumulation of stressors that have not been handled in the context of self-care.

As you proceed through life, these stressors become more and more pressing, stacking up until you reach burnout or an empty tank. In other words, take your time. When you feel like you're about to need assistance or a step back, let those you trust know. Give them time to prepare so they can respond to your outreach more successfully. Before you ask for something, pre-ask someone to accept your request for assistance, room, or time.

The Kindness Factor: Remember that people enjoy lending a hand.

Consider the last time you offered assistance or were prepared to respect someone's need for privacy. You likely left the encounter with a strong sense of fulfillment, kindness, and pride. That's because people truly enjoy lending a hand to one another. We have empathy hardwired into us, especially empaths, because we like helping one another with acts of kindness, both big and small. In fact, they occur daily worldwide.

You have many acquaintances who, if asked, would be pleased to assist you. They would have happily watched your children, helped you with a project you were stuck on, or provided you with the privacy you needed to reflect. Never was their readiness to assist you in doubt. Your anxiety and incapacity to ask were, and still are, an issue. There are people out there who wish to assist. But it would help if you let them in by opening the door. This will thrill the budding or diehard empath.

How to Take Care of Your Emotions in Tough Times

Recognize the sadness you're experiencing, avoid pretending to be happy, and remember that nothing is permanent. Clinging to anything, whether it's hopelessness and despair or our ambitions to improve the world, only leads to agony.

This too shall pass.

How to Take Care of Your Emotions

1) Connect with people who share your enthusiasm for the same subjects. Make sure you are surrounded by individuals who can empathize with you through your self-care pals, a community of care, or a local cause you volunteer for. Venting on your own doesn't work. But what if you complain and do something? There is a recipe that works!

2) Directly return positive deeds to the universe. Focus on building rapport, providing assistance, and showing the world that good deeds are still being done.

3) Carefully select how you stay informed. Consider how much news you are taking in, and be aware of its emotional, mental, and physical effects.

How to Control Tough Feelings Without Suppressing Them

The two most common responses when it comes to managing challenging emotions are to act out or to suppress. When you express a powerful emotion like rage through your actions, you'll probably experience unfavorable effects on your relationships, work, and play. When you act out, it usually has a domino effect that makes people around you angry and things more complicated. The results of holding back those powerful emotions might be even more harmful.

Many individuals are unaware of another method for controlling emotions: experiencing the experience. Like ocean waves, emotions can be compared to energy waves that vary in size and strength. Like other natural phenomena, they tend to appear and disappear quite swiftly. Several things can happen if you try to stop this process by acting out or suppressing it.

Sadly, and ironically, attempting to "talk yourself out of your emotions" frequently leads to "greater rumination and perseveration." In other words, you will continue to dwell on and hold onto the feelings you're attempting to suppress. Anyone who has received a deep tissue massage knows firsthand how the body stores repressed emotions. Suppression builds up in the body and has a variety of aftereffects, ranging from substance misuse and suicide to anxiety, sadness, and stress-related illnesses.

The Shameful Truth About Self-Care

Self-care is a sensitive subject, and that much is certain for me. I used to believe that those who practiced "self-care" were wealthy, entitled, lucky individuals who were disconnected from other people's struggles. That infuriated me. I was envious and cynical. Self-care was something for Lululemon-clad stay-at-home mothers going to Pilates instead of single working mothers like myself who were frazzled, busy, and barely holding it together.

Yes, I was one of the individuals who mocked self-care. Instead, I overworked myself, devoting all my time, effort, and focus to my job and kids, paying bills, maintaining the house, and tending to the dog until my frenzied, unstable life suddenly came crashing down. I was "downsized".

My family and I had to emigrate to another country to get this place. I loved my coworkers and worked like a madman to fix the company's money problems, but I was eventually let go. I was abruptly shaken out of a career that I believed to be my core in the course of one brief discussion.

If I am to be completely honest, when the pieces of my life crumbled, I realized that one crucial part was missing the entire time. Love for oneself was that vital component. Self-love. Ugh. Another uncomfortable topic. Even more difficult to discuss than self-care is self-love.

I still shiver when I hear someone loving themselves because it makes me feel helpless, pitiful, and exposed. You have to love the hell out of yourself because it's like an admission that you're such a loser and no one loves you. What a pitiful situation!

Whether it's sad or not, I've realized by now that everything eventually stems from loving oneself, including self-care. To take care of yourself, you must first care enough about yourself. To treat oneself respectfully, you must first realize how important you are. And for people like myself, discovering it was a difficult, drawn-out process with a great reward

Self-Care Techniques to Apply Daily

Reevaluating Self-Care in the Face of the Pandemic

Shelly Tygielski explains why it is imperative now more than ever to take care of oneself intentionally. I developed a list of the activities that would do the most good for my emotional and mental health at this time and place. It included putting on my mask before attending to my family, the community, and the globe.

I have a lengthy list of things to do. Here are the first eight items:

1. Continue my regular, everyday meditation routine. The days merge into one another, making it simple to lose sight of time; but now more than ever, my twice-daily meditation practice (20 minutes at a time) is crucial. Additionally, I can no longer use the justification, "I don't have time", because it seems like I always have time; all I need to do is practice discipline.

2. Create a schedule to keep in touch digitally. It's a good idea to see how folks we care about and don't see very frequently are doing, especially if they live far away. When speaking across time zones, it's easy to lose track of the day; it's helpful to establish regular times for checking in, hanging out, and eating "dinner" to reestablish a sense of social order.

3. Head outside. If you are fortunate to reside somewhere with parks or waterfronts accessible by bike, on foot, or both open during the pandemic, you should use this opportunity. I make it a point to get outside each day, exercise for at least an hour, then go for a barefoot stroll in the grass.

. . .

4. Permit myself to cry. This is a section from my standard self-care plan that would be suitable to move over at this time. I will occasionally experience sadness, discouragement, or outright hopelessness. Still, I am also aware that allowing myself to experience these feelings fully and focus on my suffering will let me let go of any stress or pain and let me once more see the sun shining through the clouds. No doubt I am an empath!

5. Establish a "venting hour." We've established a "venting hour" just like other families have a "happy hour." Even though it may only last for five minutes, we ensure an "airing of grievances" (much like Seinfeld's made-up holiday, Festivus). So nobody holds anything within because we will all live close together for weeks or months. I discovered that it lessens the tension buildup and ensures there isn't any hatred, which is possible for even the most charitable among us.

6. Be more selective about how frequently I get and read news and information. After realizing how I react to the news and certain speakers, I only watch 30 minutes daily and stick to a reliable news anchor and network. Otherwise, I read articles and press conference transcripts online to receive my news. I also avoid watching the news right before bed because it can make me agitated, which is not what I want.

7. Help others without sacrificing your own needs. After a few days of layoffs in my neighborhood, I began receiving emails and reading social media posts from friends and neighbors concerned about having access to food, medicine, and other necessities. I've accepted that I don't have to experience the same problems that everyone else does, which puts me in a position to help those who need it, both in my immediate community and outside it. I used my experience in

grassroots action to start the Pandemic of Love project, a mutual aid network that has linked more than 10,000 needy families with donors who can assist.

8. If all else fails, consider what I need now. When I notice that I am not feeling well physically or mentally, this is the question I automatically ask myself. I pause, inhale deeply, and ask myself what I need. I usually always discover the solution in the void.

I often find myself glancing at my list every day. It gives me solace, reminds me that I am in charge, and shows me that I can choose to be either my worst enemy or best ally in a crisis, and I go with option two. Empaths, take heed!

Four Self-Care Practices for the Workplace

We can hold ourselves back at work because we are our own worst critics. Here are four strategies to help us stop being so hard on ourselves and use everyday activities to help us unwind when stressed. Compassion for oneself is just as crucial as compassion for others. Try the following strategies if you're having trouble feeling self-compassion:

1. Treat yourself to a meal at lunch. Take a moment to reflect on the nourishment you are providing yourself when you eat. You have the authority to decide what to consume to feel good. Bonus: according to a study, when you choose healthy foods, acknowledging the good feelings they give you helps to reinforce the behavior, increasing the likelihood that you'll do so again in the future.

2. Remember that everyone feels unworthy, just like you. Keep in mind that nearly all of us have experienced "imposter syndrome". It is the anxiety of those who have been fooled into thinking they belong will someday realize their true inferiority. Remember that everyone on the team, no matter how confident they look, experiences periods of self-doubt; this is how people are by nature. You don't have to trust these notions since they are thoughts.

3. Treat yourself with kindness. Even though it seems cheesy, my business school students have found this method helpful when they become critical of themselves: picture a close friend coming to them for advice. What reaction would you have? How would you assist? What are your thoughts? How do you feel about your friend? Try answering these questions to yourself now.

4. Seek assistance. The notion that we must "be professional" - which we interpret as being stoic and handling problems on our own - has captured many people's minds. We don't consider asking for kindness or approval in this mindset. We probably wouldn't even take it. But eventually, this "I've got this" attitude starts to wear thin, and we realize that we need help to do our tasks. Try allowing someone else to be your supporter. I advise you to practice it even more if this concept alienates you. Assistance is popular! Consider your feelings when you assist others. We feel good about ourselves and connected to others when we help others. To avoid saying, "No, thanks" or "I'm alright," try saying "yes" when someone gives you something.

Key Findings

- Several techniques for self-care: For us to refuel, renew, and rewire for action, grassroots meditation activist Shelly Tygielski provides strategies to practice self-care. One is to prepare a self-care checklist with a ton of alternatives that are personalized especially for you.
- Maybe you don't feel strong enough to ask for a break, but it's important to recognize when a "personal moment" is required.
- Before you ask for something, pre-ask someone to accept your request for assistance, room, or time.

- Many individuals are unaware of any other method for controlling emotions: experiencing the experience.
- Reevaluating self-care in the face of the pandemic: Shelly Tygielski explains why it is imperative more than ever to take care of oneself intentionally.

13

KEEPING A JOURNAL

Maintaining a journal can be beneficial if you're in an abusive relationship. By keeping a journal, you can better understand your feelings and thoughts, and you may gain perspective. Additionally, it can aid in determining what to do next. It is a great practice for empaths in particular while narcissists would find it a pain.

Security first

Your risk may increase if your partner learns about your journal. So ensure that it cannot be found and read. If there's a danger your partner could hack your computer, don't use it. If you feel it's safer to go digital, use passwords to secure all files and boost security. If you use a notebook, conceal it or put it somewhere safely (like at work). You could use the paper cover of another book to hide it.

What topic should I choose?

Whatever you want. Your diary is meant to assist you in moving toward the happy and bright future you deserve, whether through recording abusive situations or poetry as a coping method. You deserve to be happy, after all.

Note the dates, times, and names of any witnesses to the abusive behavior if you're keeping a record of it. What took place? Who said what? How did it affect how you felt?

How can journaling benefit me?

You can benefit from keeping a journal about domestic abuse in many ways. It can have a variety of appearances. Nobody will penalize you for poor spelling. Therefore, you don't need to be a good writer. It is a resource you can use for practical and emotional support.

The emotional advantages of journaling

You can develop self-confidence by keeping a journal. Keeping a journal can help you regain some control if gaslighting has destroyed your self-confidence and left you feeling lost and bewildered. Even if your abuser is telling you something different, you may continue to verify that events occurred the way you recall them by confirming your account of what happened.

You can deal by keeping a journal. Keeping a journal might help you process your trauma if you cannot talk about the abuse with friends and family and are not yet ready to seek professional support. Till you're prepared for the following step, it will assist you in "getting things off your chest." Send letters. Make doodles, and create images. Do whatever you can.

THE IMPACTS OF KEEPING A JOURNAL

Keeping a journal aids in gathering "proof". Make sure you're okay with allowing everything you write to be seen by police officers, solicitors, courts, or counselors. Your diary may be used as evidence when arranging contact arrangements for your children.

You can depart by keeping a journal. Your safety plan may be kept in your journal. You might need more time to prepare to leave. However, if you have a plan, you'll be able to visualize a better future on the page in front of you. So instead of taking a single, terrifying jump, why not escape in small steps? We will stand by your side.

Always keep in mind that the abuser alone is accountable for any abuse. This is not because of you, and you are not to blame.

Key Findings

- Maintaining a journal can be beneficial if you're in an abusive relationship. You can benefit from keeping a journal about domestic abuse in many ways. It is a resource you can use for practical and emotional support. Your diary is meant to assist you in moving toward the future you deserve. Keeping a journal can help you process trauma if you cannot talk about the abuse with friends and family.
- Your diary may be used as evidence when arranging contact arrangements for your children. You might not be prepared to leave at this time, but if you have a plan, you'll be able to visualize a better future.

14

8 KEY WAYS TO LIVE AS AN EMPOWERED EMPATH

I was captivated by a journal article about how to love an empath. I agree with the author on every point she makes regarding coping with an empath. I wholeheartedly concur with Rebecca Lipman, the author, when she says empathy can be both a blessing and a curse. These are some observations on how to live as an empath, made from the perspective of someone who operates more from feelings than their thinking center.

1. Respect and value the emotional, empathic condition of consciousness.

Empaths frequently encounter criticism for their differences. The current world despises acting from the heart and discourages it. They were different and presented many difficulties. Being misunderstood by others and internalizing their judgment is simple. Most sensitive people I have met make a great effort to hide this element of themselves.

It's a characteristic of people to be empathic, and being in tune both within and externally is a gift. Good health must detect people's emotions and the tones of their surroundings. Knowing who and what poses a threat to oneself and/or one's family and others is a fundamental survival skill.

2. Differentiate between thought consciousness and empathetic consciousness.

Because they can be seen with the naked eye, day and night have a clear distinction. Since it cannot be seen, empathic awareness is far more difficult to spot. But the narcissist and/or abuser has some inkling. Only inside can it be sensed and truly experienced. Understanding the variations in empathy's mechanisms transforms negative characteristics into positive ones.

Self-knowledge is achieved through an awareness of when the mind and its thoughts predominate. Realizing the distinctions between thoughts and feelings and the internal effects of these distinctions is empowering. The powerful defensive response provided by observation allows one to stay focused rather than being pushed by energizing tides.

3. Trust your gut feeling: it is reliable.

Most empaths reject their gut feelings. Avoid doing this. Your instincts are on the money. This does not imply that the emotion can be entirely accepted or understood. The information might be lacking. However, the emotion itself is real, and a deeper communication is taking place that must be accepted.

4. Just because something can be felt doesn't indicate the observation or understanding is complete.

A major trap for sensitives and empaths is making judgments based solely on sensed observations. Communication between men and women can be just as challenging as the link between feeling and intellectual processes. Emotional and mental states are different.

Consider what your emotions may be trying to convey. Jumping to conclusions can have terrible consequences.

The information may be muddled and concealed because emotions constantly change and have a range of depths. They are adaptable and reflecting and giving it some thought will help you appreciate the details and complexities.

5. Pay attention to how your emotions change and note the major emotional states and factors affecting them.

Recognizing various emotional states and being able to relate to feelings are two of the empath's greatest strengths. This is comparable to a musician who can distinguish between numerous musical tones or an artist who can differentiate between various color tints.

Based on external factors, the internal emotional landscape can change; various individuals, places, meals, noises, smells, and more can affect the empathic response. Empathy can develop into a talent when one knows who, what, how, and why these feelings change. It permits response rather than being motivated by empathy.

6. Encourage the emotional states you desire to experience daily.

Empaths can and should take the necessary action to feel good by being receptive and understanding which internal emotional states are important. An artist knows which color combinations will result in the desired form, much as a musician learns specific chord combinations to produce particular sounds. An empath can shape their emotional landscape by keeping more of what works in their life and letting go of what doesn't.

7. Empaths can project their feelings onto others.

The majority of empaths are ignorant of the fact that being able to perceive emotions also gives them the power to protect. Whether or not someone is conscious of the influence, it still exists.

An empath can change the energetic atmosphere of a place, event, or group of people just as they can affect the emotions and moods of other people. Most empaths inadvertently engage in this. When you understand how this occurs, it makes it possible for your very presence to be a gift to others. It can even develop into a language of silence, expressing displeasure or discontentment, without uttering a word or twitching an arm.

The sensitive person gains the ability to take control of their sphere of influence and how their moods, sentiments, and emotions might affect their family, friends, and surroundings after becoming aware of this part of empathy. Because of this, empaths must awaken to their talents—honoring, respecting, recognizing, and accepting responsibility for what occurs within oneself.

8. Find artistic outlets to express yourself as an empath.

Empaths frequently feel they need to be understood and heard; many people will never comprehend this because it is an internal domain. Relying on others to help you know yourself can be both detrimental and distracting.

More importantly, empaths frequently struggle with how to communicate their spirit; thus, it's imperative to use other avenues of communication to express those feelings. Any active creation that transforms the creative source into observable effects—in writing, music, dance, or science—clears the internal channels and is self-nurturing.

Key Findings

- Respect and value consciousness's emotional, empathic condition, says author Rebecca Lipman. Empathy can be both a blessing and a curse. Most empaths reject their gut feelings; it's a characteristic of people to be empathic. Recognizing various emotional states and being able to

relate to feelings are two of an empath's greatest strengths. Reflecting and giving something, some thought can help you appreciate the details and complexities.
- Empathy can develop into a talent when one knows who, what, how, and why these feelings change. An empath can change the energetic atmosphere of a place, event, or group of people and can affect the emotions and moods of other people. Empaths must awaken to their talent and accept responsibility for what occurs within them. Find artistic outlets to express yourself as an empath.

Dear Reader,

As independent authors, it's often difficult to gather reviews compared with much bigger publishers.

Therefore, please leave a review on the platform where you bought this book.

KINDLE:

LEAVE A REVIEW HERE < click here >

Many thanks,

Author Team

CONCLUSION

A person who is extraordinarily sensitive to the emotions of those around them is known as an empath. The opposite is the narcissist. Common characteristics of empaths include empathy, compassion, and intuition. Being acutely sensitive to other people's emotional experiences has some clear advantages. You can take action to become more empathic in your daily life if you want to develop empathic abilities. Empathic persons tend to have highly charming personalities and have a remarkable capacity to attract others to them.

Narcissists typically lack empathy for others and tend to be selfish and self-absorbed. Empaths are susceptible to the emotional states of others and find it difficult to turn off these skills when another person is close by. The goal of emotional abuse, often by a narcissist, is to terrorize, dominate, or isolate the victim. Even though abuse may begin gently, it persists. Leaving an abusive relationship is the greatest option for anyone in such a situation.

Abuse can manifest itself in various ways, including physical contact through words, money, emotions, or other means of power and control. Abuse of any kind, whether it be mental, sexual, or physical, can have serious psychological consequences. It is crucial to evaluate a physical abuser's mental health and seek undiagnosed mental disorders. There is no opportunity for happiness or growth in an abusive relationship, and it is in everyone's best interest to take precautions against emotional trauma as soon as possible. Being the target of verbal abuse may be incredibly traumatic. One way is to avoid a relationship with a narcissist.

Abuse might result from insecurity or a lack of trust. To remain confident and guilt-free, verbal abuse must be dealt with as a serious offense. A support network offers a comprehensive method of treating misuse and its effects. Professional guidance can prevent the toxic environment that fosters destructive thoughts. To lessen your codependent tendencies, self-awareness and active redirection are crucial.

Art therapy has demonstrated benefits for PTSD patients by allowing patients to create and integrate. For us to refuel, renew, and rewire for action, grassroots meditation activist Shelly Tygielski provides three strategies to practice self-care. Keeping a journal can help you process trauma if you cannot talk about the abuse with friends and family. Empathy can be both a blessing and a curse, says Rebecca Lipman. An empath can change the energetic atmosphere of a place, event, or group of people. Find artistic outlets to express yourself as an empath.

www.ingramcontent.com/pod-product-compliance
Lightning Source LLC
Chambersburg PA
CBHW030301100526
44590CB00012B/477